Wrestling Legacy Data to the Web & Beyond:

Practical Solutions for Managers & Technicians

Wrestling Legacy Data to the Web & Beyond:

Practical Solutions for Managers & Technicians

P.C. McGrew
W.D. McDaniel

MC² Books
Hurst, Texas

Many of the identifiers used by vendors of software, hardware, manufactured items, services, and other products are trademarked, service marked or registered trademarks of the companies that sell them. We recognize the claims of all of the manufacturers identified in this work.

Library of Congress Control Number: 2001118531
ISBN: 1-893347-02-8
Copyright © 2001 by P.C. McGrew & W.D. McDaniel

MC² Books/ MC² Publishing is a member of the McGrew + McDaniel Group, Inc.

Jacket & Book Design by MC² Books
Jacket & Book Art by Talana Gamah

First Printing, August 2001

The authors and publisher have made every effort to ensure the accuracy of the information and examples shown in this book. However, this book is sold without any warranty, expressed or implied. Neither the authors nor the publisher will be liable for any damages caused or alleged to be caused by the information in this book. The opinions expressed in this book are those of the authors.

MC² Books are available at special discounts for bulk purchases. Please contact McGrew + McDaniel Group, 860 W. Airport Freeway, Suite 709, Hurst, Texas 76054 or call +1 817 577 8984.

Find us on the web at http://www.mcgrewmcdaniel.com/

Dedicated to our families and friends...

with special thanks to Jonathan for pitching in.

Forward

This book is born out of two previous books written in the mid and late 1980s. When we wrote *In-house Publishing in a Mainframe Environment* for Macmillan in 1985, the idea that you might use your mainframe as a publishing tool, paying attention to fonts and formatting, was quite new. The first AFP printers were new to the market and the Xerox hold on typographic output was confined to the insurance and catalog publishing industries. The idea of taking everything in the enterprise and treating it as a document was not yet fully accepted. By the time we wrote *Online Text Management: Hypertext and Other Techniques* for McGraw-Hill in 1987, mainframe-based publishing was a given in most industries, but the idea of viewing those documents on a screen instead of printing, or in addition to, printing was still foreign. Our books were published just ahead of the dawn of the Internet in popular culture, but they laid the groundwork for any company that wanted to be an early adopter.

Flash forward a decade and we are still talking about issues in enterprise printing. We've added a few twists along the way, trying to take print destined for one printer and aim it at an alternative device. Sometimes that device is a printer from another vendor, or sometimes the same vendor, which accepts a different datastream. The device may not be a printer at all. Now we take that same enterprise data and develop applications to push the output to web pages, CD-ROMs, Electronic Data Interchange formats, cell phones, and pagers.

In this book, we are going to look the legacy enterprise printing environment, with an eye toward learning all of its secrets. We want to give you the tools so that you can identify all of the parts that go into your printing today, and give you the history so that you can identify the features in your print that were encoded by your predecessors. By the end of each chapter you should know more about the datastreams, the resources, and how they work together. By the end of the book you should have all of the tools that you need to understand the migration and re-purposing issues for your environment. You should understand the questions your vendors raise, and the answers provided by the information delivery professionals in your environment. You should feel competent to migrate your print to any device or environment available today, or in the future.

To keep the scope manageable we are not covering some of the technical issues that surround moving the data. For example, we will not cover the various file transfer methods needed to move data from platform to platform in a typical enterprise. Most shops have these methods well in hand. We will also avoid the technicalities of the network requirements for moving data between platforms and the communications protocols for moving data.

And, while we wrote this book to help you get to the web and beyond, we will not cover the basics of web design or document design for the web.

To be most successful it will help to have a strategy. We can recommend another book in our series, ***Designing a Document Strategy*** by Kevin Craine, which covers this area in depth. By the end of his book, you have the tools to codify a strategy regarding your document production and the tools to sell it to your colleagues and management.

And, finally, some of this material appeared in other forms on various web sites and in articles in ***Document Processing Technology*** magazine.

Thanks and Acknowledgements

This book is based on presentations and articles we've worked on for the last 10 years, but once we started to pull it together in book form we found a hole or two that needed to be plugged. Then we needed some help to make sure we hadn't missed anything major. While we take full responsibility for what we've included and excluded, we have a group of people to thank for their input.

The biggest "thanks" go to Jeri Sampson and Phyllis Voight. Jeri Sampson, a senior programmer with IBM Printing Systems (and really a whole lot more!), has been a stalwart friend through all of our books. She gives us both the industry perspective and the IBM Printing Systems perspective. Jeri found us some of the code examples you'll see in the book. For more than a decade she's been a great friend, even when we don't get a chance to see each other very often. Thanks, Jeri!

Phyllis Voight, another long-time friend, looked at the book as a writer and editor. You always need a professional writer looking over what you produce, especially when you are a writer. Phyllis has always been willing to take a critical look at the manuscripts, even when they are in very rough form. Thanks, Phyllis!

We owe thanks to all of the folks who participate on the Xplor AFP ListServe and the Xerox ListServe. The regulars on the lists are always willing to help answer a question, no matter how obscure. Information on how to join the lists is in Appendix A. Many of the vendors who participate jumped in and provided a wealth of information, as well. While we couldn't use all of it, we provided pointers to their web sites in Appendix C. Thanks, everyone!

The basis for the list of associations in Appendix A came from fellow MC2 author Kevin Craine (***Designing a Document Strategy***). Thanks, Kevin!

Another friendly eye came from outside the electronic document industry in the person of Tim Foster, who works in Strategy & Business Development at Tri-Media Marketing (www.tri-media.com — Welland, Ontario). Tim offered the perspective of a marketing professional with little understanding of how we deal with the underbelly of the electronic document world. His insights contributed to quite of few of the re-writes. Thanks, Tim!

And, thanks to our artist, Talana Gamah, who developed our Wrestler mascot, the cover art, and the rest of the artwork in this book. Imagine getting the assignment: "Can you create a mascot for legacy data?" As always, Talana created what we needed. Thanks, also, to his partner, Ieish, who saw to it that the material got to us. Thanks, Talana and Ieish!

Pat McGrew

Bill McDaniel

Meet McGrew + McDaniel

Before you jump into the book it might help to know what it was in our background that made us write this book.

We have been business partners since 1984, with four books, hundreds of articles and three companies to our credit. In 1989, we left the warmth of an employer and formed GenText, inc., which became the primary provider of print transformation technology to document archive and other information delivery environments. We sold the company in 1998 and began pursuing consulting, speaking and writing in emerging technologies as the McGrew + McDaniel Group and MC² Publishing.

P.C. (Pat) McGrew, EDP has been active in information delivery since 1975. Trained as a journalist, she has been a broadcast reporter, print reporter, editor, and writer in a variety of industries. From 1989 to 1998 she was the President and CEO of GenText, inc., the company she and Bill McDaniel founded to develop a mainframe-based HyperText Document Management and Deployment system based on the principals defined in their first book, *In-House Publishing in a Mainframe Environment: HyperText and Other Techniques* for Macmillan. Her portfolio included the search for emerging technologies and industry trends to ensure that the GenText products remained at the forefront of the industry. Within three years from the founding of the company, GenText products provided the key piece of technology to archive vendors and printer manufacturers who required the ability to work with enterprise print files from all vendors in a seamless fashion. GenText products also provided the industry with the first print-to-view products. She developed and taught the first classes in All Point Addressable architectures (AFP, Xerox, PDF), document and GUI design for usability, tagging languages including SGML (later HTML and XML), and migration plan development for GenText customers, distributors, and OEMs.

Since the creation of McGrew + McDaniel Group she has been responsible for the development of the consulting practice and presentations on the practical applications of emerging technologies, as well as the tactical issues of working with legacy data and the Internet. M+M also provides competitive analysis and research in areas including information delivery, wireless technology, outsourcing, and emerging technologies.

W.D. (Bill) McDaniel, EDP has also been active in Information Technology since the 1975. He started as a computer operator and used that position to learn the practical requirements of data manipulation, application design, and usability requirements. Leveraging that experience, he landed at a software development company. As the Director of Research and Design he defined the architecture for one of the first variable data replacement products for the host-based printing market. From 1989 to 1998, he was the Chief Research Officer at GenText. Ultimately, GenText used their expertise in host-based and networked systems, IBM's AFP, Xerox formats, and user interface design to develop a new set of applications for transforming print files designed for enterprise printing systems into formats compatible with alternative print devices and online display technologies. McDaniel defined of the architecture to transform the complex, and sometimes proprietary, print formats.

Within three years from the founding of the company more than 20 products were being licensed to archive vendors, COLD (computer output to laser disk) vendors, application integrators, and in-house development teams on platforms including IBM mainframes, midrange UNIX systems, and networked PCs. While considered radical at the time, McDaniel's requirement to implement in the C programming language permitted rollout across a diverse set of platforms, including VM and MVS in the IBM host world, and AIX, Sun OS, Sun Solaris, OS/2, Windows 3.1/95/NT, and even MS-DOS. The modularity of the architecture made it possible for both OEM and end user implementation of complex and innovative solutions in short timeframes.

Once the architecture was refined, McDaniel pursued interests in web technology and other emerging technologies, as well as privacy and ethical considerations in computing. These on-going interests form the basis of the new consulting and strategic analysis company. In his role as Chief Research Officer for McGrew + McDaniel Group, McDaniel provides technical analysis for strategic studies, development of wireless information delivery strategies, and product development on new wireless ventures.

Contents

Preparing to Wrestle

We called this book *Wrestling Legacy Data to the Web and Beyond* because the problems you encounter in the migration of legacy print files to new output devices leave you feeling like you've gone three rounds with a Sumo wrestler. After each small success another opponent comes at you, and your options for avoiding the blows are limited.

Our goal is to give you the terminology; the background and the tools that you need to both ask and answer critical questions about your legacy print data. An additional goal is to help those of you who come to the job of migrating print jobs or the management of migration projects without the background and history that the print programmers who built your applications have had. We want you to be able to converse about the applications and the print/view issues, and really understand both the issues and the answers.

And, there are many issues. A quick look at a partial list of file formats you might encounter is enough to make you wonder about the general sanity in our industry. We are going to concentrate on just those that concern data you print today and want to re-purpose for tomorrow.

Some of the many graphic and print file formats you may encounter...

ABF - Adobe Binary Screen Font

AFM - Adobe Font Metrics File Format

AFPDS – Advanced Function Printing/ Presentation Data Stream

AI - Adobe Illustrator File Format

BDF - Adobe Glyph Bitmap Distribution Format

BMP - Windows Bitmap Format

CALS - Computer Aided Acquisition and Logistics Support Raster Format

CCITT - CCITT Group 3 and Group 4 Encoding

CDF - Common Data Format

CGM - Computer Graphics Metafile

DJDE – Xerox Dynamic Job Descriptor Entry

EPS - Encapsulated PostScript

FBM - Fuzzy Bitmap

GIF - Graphics Interchange Format

GKS - Graphics Kernel System

HDF - Hierarchical Data Format

HDS - Hierarchical Data System

HPGL - Hewlett-Packard Graphics Language

HPPCL - Hewlett-Packard Printer Control Language

HRF - Hitachi Raster Format

IMG – Xerox raster image format

IMJ - Image JPEG

IPDS – Intelligent Printer Data Stream

JFIF - JPEG File Interchange Format

LCDS – Line Conditioned Data Stream

LGO – Xerox Logo file

ODIF - Open Document Interchange Format

PCX - ZSoft Paint

PDF - Portable Document Format

PIC - Lotus PIC or Micrografx Draw

PICT - Macintosh Picture

PNG - Portable Network Graphics

PPM - Portable Pixmap

PS - PostScript

PSD - Adobe Photoshop

RAS - Sun Rasterfile

RAW - Photoshop RAW

RFT-DCA - Revisable-Form Text Document Content Architecture

RIFF - Microsoft Resource Interchange File Format

RTF - Rich Text Format

Scitex HandShake Formats

TGA - Truevision (Targa) File Format

TIFF - Tag Image File Format

TRIF - Tiled Raster Interchange Format

TTF - TrueType Font

WMF - Windows Meta File

WPG - WordPerfect Graphics Metafile

In the coming chapters you will find that we touch each of the datastreams many times as we try to build up the structure behind your legacy data. Here's the roadmap:

> We start with *The Battle Cry!* Here we look at the challenges of working with legacy data and set up definitions for the terms used throughout the book. The terminology is explained and some of the common problems get their first review.

> In *Getting Started*, we set up the plan for working through an inventory of your legacy data you have in your enterprise. This is the first of several passes through the datastreams and their resources, so be ready for a bit of repetition.

> In *Legacy Data: What's Under the Covers,* we start at the bottom of the data pyramid and look at how your legacy data got into the condition it is in. Here is where we start giving you the clues to what you really have and what to do about it.

> In *Digging Deeper*, we begin with the questions to pose before an attempt to migrate or re-purpose your data. This is the set-up for the next three chapters on the datastreams.

> In *Line Data and Line Printers 101*, the focus is the format that is still the most common print format in the world today. While AFP and Metacode are complex, line data still has the most variations and can present the most variety of challenges.

> In *All Points Addressability: IBM & Xerox*, we get into the guts of the AFP and Xerox environments. It's not a programming manual or a technical reference, but this should be enough to tell what you have, and to engage in a meaningful dialog with technicians and vendors.

> In *APA: Beyond Xerox and IBM,* we review the issues surrounding PostScript, PCL and PDF. They used to be solely desktop formats, but not they are as common in the enterprise print shop as they are on the desktop.

In *Fonts*, we look at character formats one more time, this time with the final thoughts surrounding vendor-specific fonts and target output font issues.

In *Graphics*, we identify the graphic format issues, and the challenges of taking bitmap graphics from paper to other devices.

In *Forms/Overlays*, we cover the additional challenges of working with data that incorporates electronic forms overlays and pre-printed stock.

In *A Question of Migration & Fidelity*, it's time to step up to the hard questions and start to draw a box around your viable paths to re-purposing your data. Migrate, re-format, or abandon entirely? We'll look at a couple of sample migration plans, too.

In *What's Coming in the Next Generation*, we take a short break to discuss some emerging output opportunities.

In *The Dreaded Inventory*, it's time for more lists and ask more questions. Remember, there will be a cost associated with everything you do. These lists should help you figure out what that means to your organization.

In *Trailblazers,* we look at a just a couple of quick examples of how companies have successfully moved forward with re-purposing their data. This is just so you know that you aren't alone!

In *The Appendices,* we have provided as many pointers to help that we could find.

By the time you reach the final chapter, you should be able to understand the critical success factors for moving legacy data to another platform. Whether it is another print platform or a viewing platform, we want you to be able to identify the potential problem areas. The more you know about the issues the better case you will be able to make to the executive management if you hit a snag in your migration and re-purposing plan.

The Battle Cry!

Round 1

In this chapter we cover the challenges associated with moving your legacy data to any other delivery environment. We will take a first look at:

Enterprise Print Formats: AFP, Xerox DJDE/LCDS, line data, PCL, PostScript and PDF.

Fonts: Legacy fonts and their challenges.

Graphics: Resolution and formats.

Remember, this is just a first pass through the issues. We come back to each of the datastreams, and their resources in later chapters.

You've heard the questions from managers, consultants, and industry pundits:

"Why can't we re-use the data we *already* have?"

"Why can't we view all of our documents on the web?"

"Why can't our applications talk to our PDAs and cell phones?"

" Why can't I print anything, anywhere?"

And, the dreaded:

"What can't we look at our data anywhere like they do on TV?"

The answers usually involve the words *migrate* or *transform*, which become the battle cries heard in every industry from banking to agricultural engineering. Those words, *migrate* and *transform* mean something different to everyone who uses them. For most companies it means making legacy data available beyond its typical paper delivery system, and that is not a challenge for the faint of heart.

We are going to take a careful look at all of the factors that go into a successful marriage of legacy print applications and delivery of the legacy print data using alternative means, including the web, PDAs, and even electronic ink-based devices. When you reach the end of the book you should know what you need to know to ask intelligent questions of your vendors and colleagues, as well a where to go for more help. You should even be able to interpret the answers they give you!

The simple facts in the world of corporate high-speed printing is that not everyone who works with the printers and print data has all of the terminology for all of the components of their original format or their target format at their disposal. We are going to try to help with that, too. First, we use the term *resource* throughout the book. The term *resource* is **not** universally understood, however. To be clear, we mean the fonts, forms, graphics, and print environment files that go into controlling the print job.

These resources are critical. And, no matter how many times you ask, most people do not know what resources are required for a job…even if it's in production.

What does it mean to work with legacy data and bring it to alternative platforms? Engineering the solution is different for every company, but the mechanics and tools are remarkably similar. The hundred-thousand-foot overview is that you'll need to uncover the deep dark secrets of all of your applications, then try to locate the best solutions for moving both the applications and the data they work with to the new platforms and delivery vehicles.

All the while, you'll be battling *look and feel* issues. When you move to the web:

- How close does the web version have to be to the paper version of the document?
- Can you re-design for new delivery devices, or do regulatory requirements force you to duplicate the paper version of your documents?
- How small is the type?
- What do you do about color?
- How large are the graphics?

Then, you move into even more interesting questions. What happens when you move to even smaller display devices like cell phone screens, PDA screens, or even purpose-built devices? What are your liabilities? What are your responsibilities?

Beyond the look and feel of your applications, there are the security issues and access issues that raise their heads at every turn.

About the time you think you've answered every question and encountered every problem, testing will uncover even more of those deep dark secrets. You will find graphics that were created with proprietary fonts and data that was re-mapped in COBOL, PASCAL, PL/I or even FORTRAN routines that may not move to the new platforms. The routines may be hidden in external procedures and files that hide them from view. You may even find programming written within the print applications using the printer datastream language! The older the application, the more likely it is that you'll find interesting anomalies. However, do not be surprised if you find them in even your newest applications.

If this sounds like a big job, it is. However, it is not an impossible job. Many companies have successfully moved applications originally designed for Xerox, IBM, generic line printers, and even other proprietary printers to new print environments, to the web, and beyond. They have taken many paths, and many innovations have been forged along the way. So, let's look at the tools you need to determine how to transform the output from any application so that is available for use on any delivery device, no matter how big or how small, wired or wireless.

The Problem with Legacy Data

Legacy Data comes in a variety of sizes, shapes and descriptions. It may be the output of programs written in-house over the past 30 years, the output of commercial software installed over the past 30 years, or even the output of programs written or purchased within the past few months.

Within the enterprise, it may have many personalities, especially if the corporate culture permits departments to build or buy their own application solutions. Some departments may have grown from departmental systems through mid-range systems like the IBM office systems, System/36s and AS/400s on their way to network-based printing. Others may have selected office systems from companies like Xerox, Datapoint, Data General, and Tandem, while others remained on paper until the advent of the networked PC. And, there are those who are at home on the big iron - developing all of their support applications on the IBM or IBM plug-compatible hosts.

Regardless of the pedigree, legacy data poses challenges. It is the result of the business of getting enterprise information, such as invoices, statements, specifications, policies, reports, and just about every other type of business document, through the application and print process. It may

Some Considerations

Page versus screen: 8 ½ x 11 inches and A4 are not the same as 600 x 800 or 1024 x 768 pixels.

Fonts: Proprietary formats, custom fonts, vendor-specific fonts, and how to move forward in spite of it all.

Graphics: Bitmaps, vectors, black & white, grayscale, spot color, resolution issues.

Keyboards: Keyboards in the US look different from those in Germany, the UK, and most other countries; they produce different hex values in the files, too.

be simple line data, consisting of little more than the actual text to be printed and some page eject commands, or it may have evolved to a more sophisticated form of line data that includes font calls, inserted graphics, calls to forms that overlay the data, and re-organization of the incoming data.

Beyond basic line data, there are the complex additions to line data formats, most commonly using IBM's Advanced Function Printing/Presentation (AFP) and Xerox Dynamic Job Descriptor Entries (DJDEs). The syntax for using AFP commands and DJDEs have evolved over the years, so you may find inconsistencies in coding and old syntax in your data.

Take another step and you meet the more complex forms of AFP that include composed data representations with a myriad of variations. Xerox print applications can have the appearance of full application programs or they may use Xerox's proprietary Metacode print datastream instead of or in addition to line data marked up with DJDEs.

Don't forget the data formatted for printing on PCL printers (from Hewlett-Packard or other vendors) and the data created for printing on PostScript devices or viewed in Acrobat using the Portable Document Format (PDF).

Over time, all of these formats and languages have changed.

Subtly at times, and dramatically at others, they have grown to accommodate the evolution of the languages and the devices they support. The programmers assigned to the print applications may have made changes to the base applications or written bridge code to reformat incoming data. As you can guess, they may not have documented everything they did in the rush to meet application deadlines. These things will make re-using the existing applications more challenging. This is the problem with legacy data.

A Glance toward Your Applications

Even after you identify the print characteristics of your applications, you will face the challenge of identifying the applications that produce the print and getting that old data into a format appropriate for your new output medium. Most large enterprises must still print most of their application output at some point in its life, and that print generally revolves around print formats like IBM's AFP, Xerox DJDE/LCDS, line data of all varieties, and the original desktop formats like HP PCL, Adobe PostScript and Adobe PDF.

Those applications generally use fonts with varied histories. Some of the fonts were installed with the printers and their basic programming applications as far back as the 1970s, when they were designed for use on lower resolution print devices.

One of the big problems with legacy data revolves around the fonts used to develop the original application. There is a lot more detail about font issues in later chapters, but here we want to shine a light on font basics. Without a clear understanding of what fonts the data you have expects to use, it is easy to make poor decisions about how to handle font decisions for the new delivery environment.

Why Care About Fonts?

The fonts that you use with your legacy data are files with information about how to map the data to a visual representation of the data. That representation is often specific to the hardware used for printing. When you try to migrate to new and exciting output devices it can be difficult to cause the data to appear identical to the original print because of the variations in the font file formats, their internal architectures for building the character images, and how they handle the white space between characters and between the lines.

If you are old enough to remember typewriters, you might remember the difference between Pica and Elite typewriters. If you typed a document on a pica typewriter, you saw different line endings than you saw if you typed on an Elite typewriter. Pica and Elite typewriters each use a different number of fixed characters per inch. Those problems are multiplied a thousand-fold in the world of legacy migration.

Prepare to make decisions regarding what fonts are critical to the look and usability of your documents, which have legal requirements associated with them, which have corporate branding issues associated with them, and which can reasonably change without requiring a vote of the corporate board of directors.

The Look of the Document

While one of the problems you encounter is older fonts, another potential problem area involves the graphics that populate your business documents. You may have corporate logos and product branding icons associated with processes and functions, or even signatures or text blocks that could not be rendered using a real font. Each of the possibilities has its own challenges.

One issue with graphics involves resolution. If you take a 300 dot per inch (dpi), 480 dpi, or 600 dpi graphic and put it onto a screen with an average equivalent resolution of 72, 90 or even 120 dpi and a completely different color model, the results may not be acceptable. Does that mean every graphic will need a makeover? It is definitely a possibility, but a lot depends on how the original graphics were created, if source files are available, and how much fidelity to the original is required. We look at all of this in a later section, but here we want you to understand that there will be a lot to consider.

The file formats, including fonts, graphics, electronic overlays/forms, and other resources used to create your print, are only a part of the picture. They are the biggest part, but not the only part. There is also the question of the real estate available to present your data, how it is oriented (tall/portrait or wide/landscape), and how you want to handle the navigation of the document in its new form. These are big questions because a screen of any size is not a piece of paper.

Think about that for a moment. When you look at a screen,

the proportions of height-to-width are closer to a landscape page than a portrait page. Much of the information we try to display, however, originates as a portrait printed

What to Look For...

Legacy Data: Establish a definition that you can use and explain to internal users as well as vendors and consultants.

Applications: Programs and application code come in all shapes and sizes. Don't forget to include pre-processors and post-processors on your list of applications to review.

Output: Most legacy data was designed to go to print, but archiving systems and document/report management systems may have required their own data formats. Include all of the possible existing output environments in your initial review.

page. From the start, we are going to have a challenge. You have to stop thinking in terms of 8.5 inches by 11 inches of paper real estate (or 210mm x 297mm for A4) and begin to look at the information presentation to determine the best way to migrate.

Once you understand what you have, you will move on to the process of determining the best tools for making your data available in alternative environments. There are as many approaches as there are enterprises around the world. Some of you will need a one-time conversion of all resources and programs to accommodate on-the-fly publishing to paper or screen, while others will favor an approach that reconstitutes the data for the target alternative output devices using batch transform programs. Still others will find combinations of batch and WYSIWYG (What You See Is What You Get) products, including print drivers, batch transform products and import/export schemes through document creation tools, that create the best environment.

Look at proven methodologies, whether you decide to do it yourself using in-house staff and resources, contract out to a service company, or purchase a solution from a vendor. Remember that *proven* in this case should mean that someone has used the tools to migrate or transform data that is similar to the data you are working with. This is an important point because there are so many variations in data formats, data management methodologies, and application tools.

How can you tell if it is a ***proven*** method? To start, ask potential vendors questions about who is using their method and what type of analysis was done before implementation. Be wary of anyone who tells you that it wasn't necessary to do any analysis or anyone who tells you that their method works regardless of the type of data you have. Potential solution vendors should be asking to see your data and the resources that support that data. They should be asking you about what creates it and how the data is stored. And, finally, they should be offering to run tests for you or give you enough access to their applications to run a test for yourself.

What Can You Re-Purpose?

For most companies this legacy data is the foundation of the corporate information database, which means that it has to be handled as carefully as possible. The starting point for working with it should be the identification of the applications that produce output, whether that output is printed directly from the application or passed to other programs for enhancement, re-purposing, printing, or storage.

Can any application be re-purposed for the web or some other alternative device? While you will always find situations where the cost to re-purpose the data would not be worth it, the answer is that any application can have its output re-purposed. Some applications will be easier than others, and some just shouldn't be moved. The only real requirements are that, at some point, you need access to all of the input, all of the output streams, and a way to describe and reformat the output for the new target delivery environments.

While we will talk more about moving legacy data to the web or web-enabled/web-friendly environments, the procedures we walk through in the forthcoming pages will work regardless of the actual target output environment, including cell phones pagers, and electronic ink devices.

Looking through your business applications you should find business-to-business deliverables, customer-deliverables, and internal deliverables. Some of these applications generate paper invoices, bills, and other documents that might be candidates for migration. To keep the job manageable, the best place to start is at the output end of your system applications. Start with the printers. Anything printed on green bar paper or its equivalent, as well as anything printed on a form (electronic or pre-printed) is a candidate for migration to online delivery.

What About Composition Tools?

In this book, we are concentrating on the output of the applications and tools you use, not the tools and applications themselves. That would be a separate book. However, there are a few things you will want to know about the applications you use as you create your inventory lists and do your audits.

Composition tools are that class of applications that cover mainframe and PC-based products used to add formatting information to text blocks. Composition tools come in two basic flavors: tagged/batch and What-You-See-Is-What-You-Get (WYSIWYG).

Batch tools are most commonly found on the mainframe. The most popular batch composition tools remain IBM's Document

Tagging Examples

SCRIPT:

.h1 Heading Text

.br

.p paragraph text

DCF:

:h1.Heading Text

:P.Paragraph Text

Composition Facility (DCF)/SCRIPT and it's extension called BookMaster, and a product from Document Sciences, Inc. called CompuSet (formerly XICS). You might also find Waterloo Script, which has a lot of the same history as DCF, but was developed by the University of Waterloo in Canada, and so has some different features than IBM's product. For example, it directly supported most Xerox printers early in its product cycle, while DCF requires third party add-ons to produce output to Xerox printers.

Most these products owe their existence to Dr. Charles Goldfarb, a researcher at IBM who defined the method for making content and formatting independent of each other. His original application was for legal documents, but the methodology he defined worked for business documents across the board.

In all of these products, there are sets of tags or controls that authors or document formatting specialists add to the text to cause formatting (and sometimes other processing) to occur. The tagged text files are then composed and the result is a print file.

If you still have these products in use, and many companies do, you will want to know what version and release you are using, what default fonts are in use with these products, and if you use the output of these composition tools with other applications programs.

For example, both CompuSet (which also has a visual design component) and DCF are often found in the insurance industry working in concert with a product called originally called DocuMerge (now DocuMaker) from DocuCorp. If you have applications, such as DocuMerge, that rely on composition tools, such as CompuSet or DCF, make note of it on your inventory. Also watch for products like EZ Letter, an older product in Group 1's family of products that include DOC1. It's based on tagging and for mail merging applications. If you find any merging application make note of it because there are always multiple steps to the printer.

As plans are made to re-purpose your data there may be issues resulting from which composition tool is used, or you may find that font specifications and other formatting routines are managed and specified in the composition system and not in the final application. This can make your migration easier if you have a central point of font specification for all application documents, or it can make your migration more difficult if you discover that every individual document has its own set of font specifications. Find the internal experts to help you do the inventory.

WYSIWYG tools are generally found on the PC. They may be purpose-built for a specific environment, such as a forms development tool, or they may be general-purpose word processing systems, such as WordPerfect or Microsoft Word. General purpose PC tools often require some additional tool to produce output compatible with host-based applications or to produce output to the AFP and Xerox print environments, so look for critical items like print drivers or third-party utility programs if you know that you use PC-based tools for your development.

If you are using one of a more recent class of composition tools, such as Dialogue from Exstream or Opus from Elixir, they generally provide composition, resource management, and multi-purpose output. Applications using these types of tools should migrate to the web and other devices without difficulty, but always talk to the internal experts and the vendor about how your environment is configured.

Getting Started

Round 2

By the end of this chapter, you should have a basic understanding of the types of print data that you will find in your organization and the resources that support the way they look when they print. We will take a first look at:

Output: Finding out what you really print.

Fonts and Graphic: Finding out where your resources reside and how many variations you maintain.

Formatting: Finding out what controls the formatting of the documents and where you can make changes.

Here we are getting into more depth, so read carefully!

To start the review process let's look at all of the types of output from your system applications. The best approach is to look at the current production schedules for your system printers, if you can acquire them. This should tell you what jobs are coming through on a daily, weekly and monthly basis. Remember that you will need to seek out the quarterly, yearly, and regular special jobs that occur in most shops. If you have multiple print shops on site or use remote print services you will have to get those lists as well. Do not forget the departmental printers and local printers used for regular jobs. You want to arrive at a list that includes what output is produced by which applications and who gets the paper once it is printed.

This can be one of the hardest tasks. It is common to discover that applications processing nightly, weekly or monthly are producing reports that are never delivered to anyone. You may also find reports that are printed only to go directly into a file, never to be reviewed by anyone.

Remember to check with department heads, customer liaison personnel, business analysts, call center personnel, and the various levels of managers to determine what they print regularly outside of the normal print runs, and what they would like to be able to see online instead of printing. For many it is possible to give them large amounts of square footage back in their offices and cubicles by moving to online viewing of regular print outs or archive documents.

When you have your list, it should look something like this:

Internal Print	Customer-Directed	Supplier
Cash Reports Order	Invoices	Purchase
Accounts Payable	Escrow Analysis	Invoice
Accounts Receivable	Welcome Letters	Checks
Store or Warehouse Logs Inquiry	Inquiry Responses	Inventory
Shop Floor Logs Notices	Checks	Credit
Build Reports Reports	Insurance Policies	Inspection
Inventory Reports Orders	User Manuals	Pre-paid
Payroll Reports Requests	Benefits Packages	Credit
Payroll Checks Orders	Gift Certificates	Shipping
Audit Reports Lading	Letters of Credit	Bills of
Employee Directories Invoices	Marketing Material	Pro Forma

This is not a comprehensive list, but you can see where we are heading. There is a lot of paper produced everyday in most organizations. Remember to include departmental newsletters, customer-directed marketing communications by type, and any other regularly produced communication. Your goal is the most comprehensive list you can muster. Do not worry about how long the list is, and if you feel the need to divide it into a few more categories, go ahead.

For some organizations, the table gets a bit more complicated because of the variety of print methods in use. Some printers are centrally controlled, attached to mainframe systems managed by the IT department, while others are departmental printers used for specific applications, or personal printers assigned to individuals instead of departments or applications. Printers used in the IT-controlled print room often use different print languages than the departmental printers. Personal printers may have been purchased over time and use PCL, PostScript or other proprietary languages. You will usually find that the printers each speak different languages and have different characteristics, which is part of the challenge of taking all of this data to the web. The data is usually conditioned for the target printer.

A Pass at Printer Languages

Now you want to look at the application output again, but this time to identify the output environment. The table below identifies line printers, PCL printers, AFP printers, DJDE and Metacode printers, and PostScript printers. It's a good start because it helps to identify the output language of the current data, and will help you to ask the right questions about how the data is prepared for print. It does not, however, tell you everything you need to know about the data. Each type of output has many variations, as you will see in later chapters. Remember that this is just a sample and you should see a different picture at your shop.

Internal Print	Printers	Customer-Directed	Printers	Vendor	Printers
Cash Reports	Line	Invoices	AFP or DJDE	Purchase Order	PCL
Accounts Payable	Line	Escrow Analysis	AFP or DJDE	Invoice	AFP
Accounts Receivable	Line	Welcome Letters	DJDE	Checks	AFP
Store or Warehouse Logs	Line	Inquiry Responses	PCL or PS	Inventory Inquiry	PCL
Shop Floor Logs	Line	Checks	AFP or PS	Credit Notices	PCL
Build Reports	Line	Insurance Policies	DJDE	Inspection Reports	Line
Inventory Reports	PCL	User Manuals	Meta	Pre-paid Orders	PCL
Payroll Reports	Line	Benefits Packages	DJDE	Credit Requests	PCL
Payroll Checks	AFP	Gift Certificates	PostScript	Shipping Orders	PCL
Audit Reports	Line	Letters of Credit	PCL		
Employee Directories	AFP	Marketing Material	PostScript		

Let's start getting our toes in the water by taking a quick tour of the datastreams identified in the sample table. We'll look at them all in more detail later, and you may already be very familiar with one or more of them. If you are already comfortable with the basics of the datastreams, go ahead and skip forward to the next chapter.

Each datastream carries information about the print environment, the data, and the resources required to print that data on the target output device in the desired format. That means that the datastream designed for print carries a lot of stuff your web browser will not understand at all.

In fact, it carries a lot of information even another printer might not understand.

Here are the basics for each environment. In later chapters we cover them in more depth, but to set the baseline, this is what we mean when we refer to the datastreams.

Line Printer   Those devices that look or behave like very fast typewriters. These are often found on shop floors, in back offices, or in the IT print room churning out boxes of print each day. They may use print chains, daisy wheels, moving balls, lasers, or even inkjet technology. What they have in common is that the data that is passed to them includes control characters to tell them when to advance the paper, when to overprint to create bold type, and even when to change typefaces on printers that support it. Line print can also be fed to Xerox DJDE/Metacode printers, AFP printers, and most other printers as long as the proper commands precede the data. This is where it gets interesting. Industry estimates indicate that most printing done today is still conditioned for line printers, even though it may be heading for a more sophisticated device.

AFP   Advanced Function Printing/Presentation was architected by IBM Printing Systems and is used by IBM and a number of other printer manufacturers to drive printers at the high, middle and low-end of the print speed range. AFP has both the advantage and disadvantage of being all things to all people. It can handle plain line data conditioned with carriage controls or it can understand controls that condition line data with objects that format the line data. In its more sophisticated forms, it can be a structured file format compatible with applications generally found in large mainframe environments. It also has formatting characteristics that are at home with PC/Network, AS/400 and UNIX environments. Using AFP structures, you can change fonts, add electronic forms, and even perform conditional processing or switch output bins at the printer.

IPDS   Intelligent Printer Data Stream. We're adding this here because IPDS is the language actually used by AFP printers. AFP is produced by your applications, but it is then passed to the IBM Print Services Facility (PSF) or comparable program to be conditioned for a specific output device. Sometimes users are confused about what IPDS is and what you can do with it. We recommend that you work with AFP rather than IPDS since IPDS is device-specific. There are some companies that provide IPDS solutions. If that is what you believe you must have, be sure to have a long discussion with your vendors.

DJDE   Dynamic Job Descriptor Entry coding is found on Xerox printers. DJDEs are used to condition line data for printing by invoking electronic forms, changing fonts, adding graphics, and even manipulating the position of the data on the page.

Metacode   Xerox Metacode is a proprietary language developed by Xerox to control their high-speed print environments beyond the capability of the DJDE language. Metacode is most often the output of applications in the insurance and financial markets, but some brave end users have created Metacode-producing engines as well.

PCL   The Printer Control Language was defined by Hewlett-Packard and extended by many other manufacturers. PCL strikes fear in the hearts of many who work in datastream transforms because there are so many variations. It supports older style printers with cartridge fonts, color and multi-tray/multi-bin devices. PCL is as sophisticated as the AFP and Xerox environments.

PostScript   The Adobe-defined languages for highly graphic print environments has evolved down several paths. PostScript supports the advertising and media print market as well as the business printing market. PostScript comes in several levels of supports and there are OEM-specific extensions and enhancements.

PDF   Portable Document Format (PDF) provides display support for PostScript, and is becoming the standard for online viewing and electronic book delivery.

That's the landscape. Data in many variations. It is important to remember the type of data you are working with as you move forward with your plans since each print language has its own type of resources, such as fonts, graphic file formats, and page formatting resources.

Formatting Fundamentals

The next step is to look at the nature of the print and what it looks like to the naked eye. You need to understand the overall formatting of the output, including the orientation of the print on the page. Are you working with applications that print one-side only in portrait orientation (print along the narrow axis of the page)? Do you also have landscape print (print along the wide axis of the paper)? Do some jobs print in a mix of landscape and portrait?

Do you have documents that print in tumble format, where the back of the sheet prints 180 degrees in orientation from the front so that the document is bound at the top and can be read by lifting the pages? Extra-wide? Extra-narrow? Two-up? Four-up? Duplex? Letter or A4? Monarch? Did someone decide to have a custom size paper made? If it's getting a bit scary, that's understandable.

Part of the problem is that the data was formatted to fit on that piece of paper, with specific margins using fonts, line spacing, and resources designed for a specific print environment. Now you need a plan that gets that data, even the data that is printed upside down, into a format that can be read on a screen. Depending on how the data is generated and formatted in the datastream, this could be a major problem.

As crazy as it may sound, we have seen programs written to place every other line of data backwards because a programmer in the distant past thought it would make the printer print faster. We've seen applications that call for inverse portrait fonts and print the data upside-down, too. Even today, talented print programmers often manipulate text strings and place them into the print output to meet a specific customer demand. Sometimes those manipulations narrow your options for re-purposing the print output.

And, what about documents that have portrait and landscape print on the same page? Not many of us have those monitors that turn on an axis. Even if we did, which way would we turn it? Beyond the questions of orientation, there are the issues of fonts, typefaces, inter-character spacing, kerning, and line spacing.

The fonts that you see representing the characters on a page contain encoding that the print device uses to identify the name of the font and to locate its font file. From the font file the device derives the information about the characters, their spacing characteristics, and the language information necessary to ensure that when you type a specific letter on your keyboard you get the character you intended. Font mapping is performed on the print device, in the print file, or somewhere else that is accessible to the print environment. If everyone played by the same rules and the entire world used Arial and Times you wouldn't have these challenges. In fact, for every type of printer and print file format there are font file formats that go along with them.

The trend toward standard font formats like Adobe Type Manager (ATM) and TrueType or OpenType provide some consistency in the PC and Network world. But, back at the IT center, that standardization is still working its way into place.

The Font Story Continues

- Fonts may share a name and not be the same
- Fonts may be characters or contain graphics
- Pay attention to the age of the font files
- Look for evidence that the fonts have been edited
- Remember that fonts are licensed

There are still many line print devices sold every year since they meet all kinds of needs. If you look carefully at most line print devices, they support only a very few typefaces. Many of them look familiar to those of us old enough to remember manual typewriters and the very earliest office word processors. Common font names include Prestige, Gothic, Elite, and Courier. So common, in fact, that when IBM introduced its first high-speed laser printers they made sure to provide compatible fonts for those line printer applications to make it easy for their customers to move up to laser printing.

A word of caution, however. Fonts that share the same name do not always share the same characteristics. Line print devices were originally created using mono-space type — each character was the same width. Look at the width of the letter *w* and the letter *l*, and you get an idea of what that meant. It made printing columns of numbers a breeze because everything lined up.

On the original line print devices the characters were on a print chain or ball, ensuring that all of the characters were identically spaced. When you try to move these applications to high-speed laser printers or on to the web and its sister display environments, you face the lack of true mono-space fonts. That means that columns of numbers may not line up correctly, and text targeted for specific locations in a pre-printed form might end up in the wrong place entirely. Any application that relies on the mono-space nature of the fonts to space the text becomes a potential problem.

Some of those applications may have fought this battle already. When applications migrated from the older style mechanical line printers to high-speed printers, like the old IBM 3800 printers and their emulations, or the original Xerox ESS printers like the 8700 and 9700, they usually required modifications to use the fonts designed for these new devices. The fonts with the same names shared many characteristics with their older cousins, but they were not identical matches. The new laser printer fonts could match the size and shape of the characters, but the inter-character spacing and inter-line spacing, as well as the size of the space invoked by a space key, all varied. The resulting fonts were often called pseudo-monospace fonts.

Many applications were modified to take advantage of the new fonts and character sets by redesigning the applications to use the pseudo-mono fonts and proportional fonts to achieve a more appealing look. If the migration strategy in previous years allowed for changes to the programs to take advantage of the fonts designed for the printers you will find applications calling for mono-space or proportional fonts with names like GT20, Pi and Specials, or Sonoran Sans Serif in the IBM world. In the Xerox world, you find names like UN111E or P0612B. There are thousands of applications running in print shops throughout the world using these fonts everyday. None of these fonts has easy equivalents on the web.

If you have applications built in the past 10 to 15 years, you may also find that the font calls include Helvetica, Century Schoolbook, Times New Roman, and other familiar looking names. Take care. Once again, the font name may not be the key. For any document where the formatting is tight and relied on the *font metrics* (how the characters were spaced, how white space was applied between characters and lines), you may be in for a rude surprise. Sometimes fonts with the same name behave differently between printers that are sitting next to each other because they were purchased from different font houses, purchased at different times,. And, since it is possible to edit fonts in both the IBM and Xerox printing environments, it's not unusual to find that characters were deleted or added to fonts.

A key piece of information is that in the IBM world, as on your PC, the font files remained on the host computer. In the Xerox world the fonts live directly on the printer's hard drive, similar to cartridge fonts on older desktop printers. Especially in the Xerox environments, it is common to have different fonts on each printer in the shop. You might find eight printers, sitting side-by-side on the print shop floor, and no two with the same fonts available to them.

The IBM print environments are generally more centralized because they use font libraries, but even in those environments there are often a variety of font libraries and differences in individual fonts within those libraries.

The important thing to remember is that fonts are going to be an issue as you move forward. If you can collect a list of every font available on all of your printing devices, and a list of those actually used, you will be in great shape. Sadly, font management software is rare and shops with that key information are few in number. If you are one of the lucky ones, congratulations!

Oh, one more word. Fonts do not always mean typefaces. In the world of enterprise printing, there are thousands of instances of graphics being encoded as fonts. Sometimes they are signatures, sometimes they are corporate or departmental logos, and sometimes they are illustrations. Look around for these. Many were created because the first generations of laser printers were not ready to deal with large bitmap graphics. Many print programmers became proficient at designing fonts and adding the programming to print applications to use those fonts. The payoff was a more sophisticated looking document that didn't slow the printer to a dead stop the way many bitmap graphics could.

Graphic Tidbits

- Black and white or color, raster or vector
- Proprietary formats and industry standards
- Source files on hosts, networks, and workstations

Like fonts, graphics in the enterprise printing world have evolved. At the PC level, you may have bitmap BMP and TIFF files, but in enterprise printing you are more likely to see PSEG (IBM AFP Page Segments) files or Xerox LGO (logo) or IMG (bitmap image) files. There are enhancements to bitmap formats to add spot color and full color in both Xerox and IBM environments. And, for the most part, those file formats do not directly translate to the web formats like JPEG, GIF, or PNG, though applications developed in the late 1990s may incorporate JPEG and GIF formats with wrappers that explain them to the existing print environments.

As you did for fonts, make a list of the graphic formats in use in your target applications. You might find that many of them began on PCs and have an easy path to re-creation in a web-friendly form. Others may be the result of mainframe-based programs. Start by identifying which applications use graphics as part of the output. Remember that a graphic might exist as a font, as we said earlier. Start with a table that looks like this:

App. Name	Graphic / Location	Created Date	Font/FONTLIB	Created Date
Customer Production Monthly Stmnts	Map1.pseg / Production Lclsvc.pseg / QA1 Lclsvc.pseg / Test3 Splsh.pseg / Test3		Pressig.font3820 / Production	
Customer Invitation Letters	Map1.pseg / Production Bjones.pseg / Production Flower.pseg / Production		Pressig.font3820 / Production Bjonessig.font3820 / Test Bjonessig.font3820 / QA3	

In the IBM and network printing environments, the resources are normally located in directories on a network drive or mainframe disk. The name is important, but don't forget the location and creation dates. These may become critical pieces of information if you discover multiple copies of the same graphic or signature file. List everything you find and mark those that you believe are the production copies.

This may take a bit of detective work. We have found situations where production graphic files were being pulled from private datasets in mainframe environments, and from personal workstations in network environments. Needed changes were applied to the production libraries, but those changes failed to appear during testing. Several days of tracking down the program modules and reviewing the code located a block labeled *temporary patch* added four years earlier. It directed the program to pull the resource from the private dataset for testing. The follow-up movement to production had never happened.

It can happen in Xerox environments as well. Graphics can reside on the printer's hard drive, or in host or network directories. Knowing which versions of the graphics are on each printer can be a challenge. In most environments there is no automatic resource management, only the directory lists.

Forms and Overlays to Format your Data

- Electronic file containing boilerplate information
- May contain text, graphic or image
- Often used in data merging applications
- Sometimes used in electronic form-fill applications
- A discrete resource; format varies by datastream
- May be embedded in the datastream: inline forms
- May be referenced: external forms

We have mentioned forms and overlays. At this point in the process start thinking about all of the applications that use pre-built electronic forms. Those forms may be created using any number of applications and may be created on any platform. The important thing will be to understand where all of the forms are used, how they are created, and what resources the forms use. Remember, they can use fonts and graphics that are not the same as the base applications. We'll repeat this caveat several times because it is a common problem during the testing phase of a migration. You moved everything correctly, but the output is just not correct. That's when you discover that the electronic forms overlays use slightly different logos and signature fonts, but they use the same file names as the base applications.

Summary

If the challenge is to make the corporate data more available and accessible, the wars will be fought on battlefields of fonts, graphics, electronic forms, and the very subjective nature of what looks good on a screen. In the following chapters we will look at each issue you will face and provide the information you will need to ask good questions, understand the answers, and make the best decisions for your companies enterprise environment.

Legacy Data: What's Under the Covers?

Round 3

By the end of this chapter you will know more about the structure of the data in your environment and the types of applications that generate it.

> **Data:** ASCII, EBCDIC, ANSI, UNICODE.
>
> **Print Formats:** Line Data, AFP, Metacode, DJDEs, PCL, PostScript, PDF.
>
> **Resources:** Fonts, Forms, Graphics, Control Files.
>
> **Output:** Print, CD-ROM, Web, Cell phone, Pager, Electronic Ink, Billboard

Here is where we start to build a set of best practices.

To get a good grip on the world of legacy data it helps to have some of the history behind the data. If your background is in computer science, you might find some of the information to be very basic. For those who came into the world of legacy data by alternative routes, this section is designed to put your data into perspective, and to help explain why there is so much to be concerned with when migrating the data to new output environments.

The Big Picture

Transform	Transform programs re-format data for new output media
Format	Print programs format information for print devices
Application	Applications manipulate data to create information
Programming	Within the Programming layer hex values are translated to ABC's
Encoding	Within the operating system 1s and 0s translated to hex values
	Binary data stored as 1s and 0s deep in the computer

Data comes in layers. At the base is the binary data. Sitting on top of that base are layers that act as translators that make the data usable, first to programs, and finally to you and your users.

Deep in the heart of all computers the data lives as groups of 1s and 0s. But, that is not what you see on paper, and that is not what you see on a screen. Except for some hardy souls who do deep machine-level programming, those groups of 1s and 0s remain hidden from view by a layer of technology that makes programming and data manipulation easier. It also facilitates the human-computer interaction. Think of the 1s and 0s as on and off switches for electrical circuits. That was their original function.

The layer that hides those 1s and 0s is an encoding layer, which acts as a liaison between the binary layer and the programming layer. The encoding layer maps the deepest level of machine code to something more manageable. Over time, a variety of paths evolved, and they each have their own tables and mappings that apply. You will not generally need to translate data at this level. However, we argue that it is important for anyone embarking on a migration to new output devices to understand what lies behind the data so that when you see at-signs (@) appearing instead of spaces you can immediately identify the problem as being in the code translation. An @ is an EBCDIC 20. If you send a bunch of ASCII space values (ASCII Hex 20) to an EBCDIC environment, you get the @ instead of the space.

It would be wonderful if the early developers had all agreed on a standard and stayed with it, but like most facets of our world, this is not the case. Hex formats come in two basic flavors: ASCII and EBCDIC. You generally find EBCDIC originating on IBM mainframes and ASCII originating in network environments, including the many flavors of UNIX.

ASCII has some variations as well. There is the basic 7-bit representation that print programmers learn when working with Xerox printers. Then there is the ANSI 8-bit code that adds special symbols. If you use Windows-based programs, look at the character maps for the normal text sets. You'll see the additional 128 characters that 8-bit code representation provides.

However, we live in a world that speaks more than just English and uses more than a basic roman character set. There are hundreds of languages and dozens of character sets. After all, a Š is a valid character and requires representation! That led to Unicode, a 16-bit code that goes beyond the basic ASCII limitation of 255 character forms to 65536 character forms. You'll find that font families in most print environments are now also available in Unicode

Building Data Layers

EBCDIC Value	Space	ASCII Value	Space
EBCDIC HEX	40	ASCII HEX	20
Binary 0100 0000			

character sets, but legacy data was most often created before Unicode. This means that there is an opportunity for character collision as you migrate into new environments.

Character collision? That's what happens when some character or symbol represented in the original data uses a non-standard hex value. Non-standard because the original fonts and character sets did not use it, but a problem now because it is used in Unicode to represent some other character or symbol. You find it in environments where programmers used font manipulation programs to insert special characters, such as pieces of logos or character variations, into standard fonts. Later we'll cover more on the solutions to these types of problems. For the moment, just be on the lookout for these situations in your data.

Many Flavors of Data

Binary Data: Machine-level 1s and 0s.

EBCDIC: Extended Binary Coded Decimal Interchange Code; 8-bit code used by IBM mainframes

ASCII: American Standard Code for Information Interchange; 7-bit code that represents letters of the alphabet, numerals, and other symbols.

ANSI: 8-bit code where the first 128 characters are the same as the ASCII characters. The last 128 characters are used to represent special symbols. Used in Windows.

UNICODE: 16-bit code that developed to represent characters in all languages. Can store 65536 values.

Next is the programming layer. We identify it separately from an application layer, because with basic tools programmers can manipulate data and format print. It is very common in IBM mainframe environments, as well as many UNIX environments, to find print programs that establish control characters, table reference characters, and font index bytes handling, as well as rudimentary formatting for line data applications.

At the application formatting and transform layers additional encoding may exist to provide information to output devices such as high-speed printers, desktop printers, or a wide variety of other display devices including pagers, PDA's and telephones. For legacy print this usually means line data, conditioned line data using IBM Advanced Function Printing/Presentation or Xerox LCDS, or more sophisticated formatting using the full power of AFP or Xerox Metacode. In newer enterprise applications, this may include PostScript, PDF and PCL.

For most of the work that you will do to move your legacy output to new devices you will be concerned with the application and programming layers, since that is where the bulk of the formatting, font, graphic, and other resource information is located.

Where does Legacy Data come from?

Legacy Data is the result of all of the years of doing business. Even if your enterprise is only a few years old, the nature of the data, the software, and the hardware may have changed one or more times. For companies that have decades of business history, the business processes have changed many times as new business processes and systems have been implemented, and then replaced. One look at your company history will give you a good idea of how much legacy your data may be carrying with it.

When business was conducted by entering accounting information into ledger books, taking orders in order books, writing receipts in receipt books, and reconciling all of the paper at the end of the month, quarter, or year, the most successful companies were those that built efficient, consistent ways of moving corporate information. Whether they were moving information among the enterprise departments or passing the relevant information to suppliers and customers, the goal was to move data without information loss.

We tend to think of legacy data as old computer data in arcane formats, but we can take it back a few dozen steps. A look back into pre-history shows us sealed clay jars with replicas of livestock, produce, grain stalks, dry goods, and luxury goods used by merchants to document what they were sending to buyers in foreign ports. When the goods arrived at their destination, the buyer would break open the jar and match the count of the merchandise with the count of the replicas to ensure a complete delivery. The first legacy data migration was from clay replicas to images of the goods, and ultimately to numeric counts combined with a written language to represent the transmittal of goods among merchants. Business people have always contended with legacy data!

Roll the clock forward a millennium with businesses emerging from the Industrial Revolution looking for any way to gain efficiencies in production and accounting. Computers developed in academic and scientific settings, ultimately found their way into the business process.

By the middle 1960s, computing devices and the applications that ran on them were a significant factor in how large enterprises performed basic business functions. The applications created from that point forward generated files of information emanating from a variety of programming languages . They digested input data and produced output, usually to a print queue. If you work for a company with a long commercial history, you might still find programs that date back to this era.

The application programs may have been written by in-house staff, outside contractors, or purchased commercially from vendors like IBM, the old Digital Equipment Corporation (now a part of Compaq), one of the many companies that are now a part of Computer Associates, or a variety of specialty software suppliers.

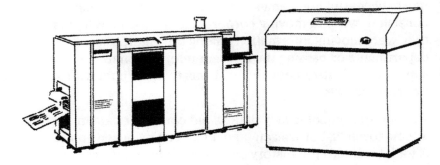

Once put into production, these programs may have been maintained on a regular basis or never touched again, depending on the function they served and the data they handled. Depending on what equipment and operating system they were written for, they produced output in either EBCDIC or ASCII text, normally destined for line printers that understood a fixed number of characters per line and a fixed number of lines per page.

While it might sound as though all of the print should follow the same basic protocols, the lesson of history is that legacy documents actually emerged in a wide variety of incompatible formats. As mentioned earlier, you have EBCDIC data generated from IBM mainframe environments, and ASCII data generated from the original midrange systems, workstations and networks. The

Formats

ASCII and EBCDIC line data; Formatted and unformatted
AFP (IBM): 3800 style/26 CCW, 3820 style/CCU, AFCCU/AFIG
Metacode/DJDE/LCDS (Xerox)
UDK/XES (Xerox)
SGML; HTML; DHTML; XML
PDF (Adobe): 1.1, 1.2...
PostScript (Adobe): level1, 2, 3...
HP-PCL (Hewlett-Packard): 1, 2, 3, 4/5, 6
Image formats: TIFF, PCX, bitmap/raw raster...

manufacturer the company settled on to meet their original data processing needs defined the nature of the data.

Over time, the applications that generated the plainest line data were often enhanced to add the ability to indent text or make it bold. How fancy they could be depended on the nature of the output device and the ability of the programmer to pass commands to the printers to get the formatting they wanted from the device.

Programmers are generally up to the challenge of making the machines do what they want. They are often very creative in how they approach the formatting challenges posed by pre-printed forms and the needs of a diverse user community.

The First Migration...

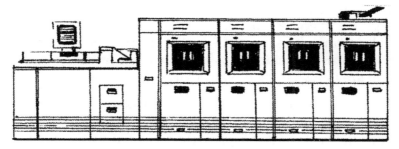

The first stage of migration of your legacy data may have occurred 20 years ago when IBM was introducing the 3800 high-speed laser printer and the original office imaging systems for word processing applications. Xerox was toe-to-toe with them in introducing their own range of office word processing systems and smarter printers including the original 8700 ESS systems and the Xerox XES printers. If your company wanted to take advantage of the features of the new printers, a little bit of programming was in order.

Some companies took this opportunity to rewrite applications from the ground up, but they were rare. Most companies settled for adding a few commands into their print routines and applications, and kept on going. As new generations of printers came along with more features, including input and output bin control, a few more print commands were added to the aging applications.

If a truly new device entered the environment, it was time for some tough decisions. Do you rewrite the application, or write a post-processor to make the data compatible with the new device? For most companies, the post-processor path became popular as the source code became more delicate and the cultural history behind the source code began to fade. By the early 1990s, it was possible to purchase commercially supported program products to convert print files from almost any format to almost any format, as long as you could identify the print environment components. Programs to transform data into new formats *on-the-fly* entered the scene, allowing delicate application programs to remain untouched while providing the needed support for new output devices.

Legacy data is the product of years of doing business and the requirement to produce printed output to support the business. It comes from old mainframes, new mainframes, old networks, and new networks. If your company has been through an acquisition or two, it may come from systems that are foreign to those you are used to working with.

Legacy data and the applications that generate it remain with us because they are ingrained in the business process. Sometimes the cost to replace the programs with more modern applications is too high. In the power management, utility management, and financial management sectors the risk of altering or replacing a key program may be greater than the companies can justify.

Looking for Clues

Working with any type of data with the intent to change its output characteristics requires equal parts of detective work, universal translation skills, and the ability to weather frustration. As you start looking at the data and the applications that generate it, you will discover the shortcuts taken to meet pressing deadlines. IT's there in the formatting coded into the applications, often using syntax and commands that work only in narrowly defined environments. You will encounter the standards that changed during the lifecycle of the data, as well as interesting bridges that worked around specific problems.

Be prepared to find everything from font information coded into application programs, to bin and tray commands grafted onto the output by staff-written post-processors. Remember that some print programs were designed to produce output to continuous rolls of paper, while others were designed for cut sheet reams of paper. This changes the page real estate available for printing, which in turn plays a roll in the orientation of the data on the page. Even issues like pagination (page numbering) and single-sided (simplex) versus two-sided (duplex) printing might be encoded in the data instead of the formatting programs.

Issues in a Nutshell

Fonts

Page orientation and dimensions

Page margins

Pagination/imposition

Data and file formats

Graphic formats

ASCII Vs EBCDIC for host-originated data

File movement and transformation

Remember that you may already have transform and conversion programs in use without realizing it. If you know that your organization has mainframe, midrange, and PC/Network applications, look for the places where they might share data and you may find an existing transform program. Look for staff-written programs that change ASCII to EBCDIC or EBCDIC to ASCII. Be prepared to discover that they do not always translate correctly, or that they have been wrong for years and there is a secondary patch program that runs later in the process to correct the output.

None of this is unusual or unique to your environment. How you approach resolving the issues you encounter will determine how successful you will be.

Don't Forget the Emerging Technologies

New technologies for presenting data are emerging daily as the cost to build convenient devices and powerful support networks falls. The earliest versions of many PDAs and other handheld devices, including cell phones, used non-standard languages to drive the information to the screen. That eliminated the issue of driving your data to those devices, except in very rare cases where marketing agreements and dedicated programmers took care of massaging the data into the required format.

All of that has changed with the move to standardize around tagged languages such as the HyperText Markup Language (HTML), eXtensible Markup Language (XML), or display languages such as Adobe's Portable Document Format (PDF). When the devices use standard interfaces it opens the possibility of driving all types of data to the screen.

If you work in an environment where customer care is an issue, pay close attention to the emerging pocket devices. Whether your customers are internal or external, the faster their questions are resolved the happier they are. Imagine the world where you can check the status of the print jobs you are responsible for by logging on to a secure web page on your handheld device from anywhere in your building, and perhaps anywhere in the world! Need to check the layout? No problem! Click on the print job name and the PDF image displays. Some companies are doing it today, and your company might choose to do it tomorrow!

To move into the world of delivery to these devices requires an additional level of complexity in document tagging and

Other Output Environments

Audio (AutoPC, Palm Pilot audio)
eBooks
PDAs and other handheld computing devices
Cell and satellite phones
Text Pagers
Information appliances and netpliances
Electronic Ink devices

handling. The more you know about the documents you have today, how they were built, how they are configured, and what it really takes to make them print, the more likely you will be to get them on to new output devices.

Remember that every move to support a new output environment has a cost associated with it. Re-purposing legacy data to create documents compatible with new delivery media requires training in sophisticated document creation and maintenance techniques, and a recognition that the tools and techniques are still in their infancy. New tools and new standards emerge regularly.

Even standards pose a challenge, though. Standards like XML are under constant pressure to admit enhancements and attach support standards. They offer power and flexibility. They also tend to provide the best chance of keeping up with the emerging devices. With power and flexibility comes a level of sophistication that requires time and effort to understand, so if you are looking at these output devices as part of a future strategy, remember to allow time and budget for the education and training you will need.

While you are looking at emerging technologies, take a look at the world of data mining and the tools that support data mining from existing text files. There are transforms and data mining utilities that can provide access to a world of information that already exists in the enterprise files, but which are hidden from view and accessibility by the print structures embedded within them. As new tools emerge that can separate the structures from the data, new sources of information become available that can be used for trend analysis, marketing, and product development.

One Last Point

The good news is that nothing is impossible! Trailblazers, early adopters, and even more conservative enterprises have done everything we talk about in this book.

The not-so-good news is that moving legacy data to any new medium requires careful evaluation of existing environments and a clear plan. Getting to a plan is the biggest challenge in most organizations.

The bad news is that the failure to evaluate and set a plan can cost time and money, and ultimately market share. In the new millennium, companies that have been in business for more than 100 years are no longer safe from bankruptcy. Companies that have been in business for more than 50 years can no longer assume that they own their market and that they have nothing to fear from the emerging markets. A quarter of a century of business no longer guarantees that your customers will remain out of a sense of loyalty. A decade is only ten years, and the last ten years has seen us move from client server applications on dedicated networks to worldwide data sharing via the Internet backbone.

The best practice is to learn as much as you can about what you have, and prepare for the future.

Digging Deeper

Round 4

It's time to come back to the print data and begin to ask the important questions about what you really have.

Resources: Fonts, Graphics, Forms.

Documents: What are they and who owns them?

Start building your own lists because here is where you start to fill them in.

Now that you know why legacy data comes in many variations, the important question is, "What type of legacy data <u>do you have</u>?" In most environments the answer is that you have several types, all with different histories and configurations.

You must determine where your legacy data came from, and what applications were used, or are still used, to generate the print files. Were the programs written by an in-house staff, an on-site contractor, a custom programming house on an outsource basis, or were they purchased from a vendor?

The answers will help you to determine how much control you have over changes that might be needed to meet your re-purposing needs. At the very least, it gives you an idea of who to talk to if you run into problem. Remember, though, that some of these programs may be 25 years old or older. The programmers or vendors may no longer be around for you to talk to, and they may not have left much documentation to help you through the difficult times.

The Many Forms of Legacy Data

Line Data

- o What type of carriage control?
- o Print conditioners?
    - EBCDIC Line Mode Data with carriage control (machine, ANSI)
    - EBCDIC Line Mode Data without carriage control
    - EBCDIC Line Mode Data enhanced with AFP X'5A controls)
    - EBCDIC Line Mode Data enhanced with Font Index Bytes FIB)
    - EBCDIC Line Mode Data with Page Definitions, Form
                    Definitions, Conditional Processing
    - EBCDIC Line Mode Data with Xerox DJDE
    - EBCDIC Line Mode Data with Xerox Metacode
    - ASCII Line Mode Data with carriage control
    - ASCII Line Mode Data with Xerox DJDE
    - ASCII Line Mode Data with Xerox Metacode
    - ASCII Line Data with HTML tags
    - ASCII Line Data with vendor-proprietary tags or other markup
    - ASCII Line Data with XML tags using an industry standard DTD
    - ASCII Line Data with XML tags using a vendor proprietary DTD

AFP print streams

- o 3800-style AFP
- o "Home made" AFP
- o MO:DCA or MO:DCA with ACIF

Xerox print streams

- o Line data with DJDEs
- o Metacode
- o Mixed
- o UDK/XES

XML, HTML, SGML and variations

PCL

PostScript/PDF

You will also want to understand the plan for using the legacy data in new applications. Is the data being migrated to a new format permanently, or is the intent to continue using the legacy applications for print and re-purposed forms of the data in the new medium? Answer this question early in the process. It can influence the decisions you make regarding fonts, graphics, and fidelity to the original print look and feel.

As you begin to look at the applications that are targeted for use beyond print, those tables we started earlier become very important. For each application, you need to know what resources are used to accomplish the printing of the final output.

Are there external resources? These files are not part of the original data or part of the application program, but called in using a pointer to another file to supply font information, graphic images, electronic overlays, and sometimes conditional processing information and formatting. If so, where are those resources located and how are they integrated with the print?

You may discover that all of the graphics, fonts, and other information are actually located entirely within the print file. This is not normally the case, but in some application situations it happens. If this is what you find, how big is the file? Why is the file constructed as a monolith, and what are the implications for moving the file to a web environment or other output environment? Large print files may contain data pertaining to a number of customers, vendors, or accounts that would be inappropriate to distribute. A file such as this might require a post-processing program to split the file apart, in addition to a transform from the print format to new media formats.

Watch for the things that tend to escape the initial analysis. Look carefully at the actual, printed output of the application. What do you see that might not be obvious from looking at the application programming and print file formats? Is there a special form that is pre-printed, an odd paper size, or a special paper stock? Where does that piece of information about the print job reside? Is it somehow encoded in the print program, or is it just cultural

Background Information

- Pre-printed stock
- Odd paper sizes
- Environmental info

knowledge that relies on the printer operators to ensure that the correct forms are loaded.

When you discover pre-printed stock, remember that the print application does not have the information available to it that is printed on the form. How can you get that information available to the new media output environment? Is it available in a print file somewhere?

This is a lot of information to stay aware of, so it will help if you start by working through the application and establishing a baseline for what you know. Then go back and ask more questions to build up your knowledge base.

Font and Graphics:
What Questions Do You Ask?

For every line of text you see on a document that prints in your environment there should be a reference to a font file (or set of related files) that causes the image to print as you see it. As noted earlier, the fonts in use may not have counterparts in display environments like web browsers. Every vendor used their own font standards, and made their own deals with font providers.

Before you get too deeply into the issue of fonts, it is worth asking the people who own the documents you will be working with if the fonts in the documents must be exact matches when you move to your new output media. In some industries there are legal issues surrounding the fonts and formatting of documents. The regulations can be so specific that if there is any change at all, including margin changes, size changes, or text re-flows because of a change in a font, the document must be submitted to a state or federal agency for re-approval. That process can take some time and may have other costs associated with it. If you work in an industry with these types of restrictions, find out how much room you have to make changes before you begin the project.

If, on the other hand, there are font requirements in place that were determined as part of a corporate branding, there may be room for negotiation when it comes to matching fonts or developing alternatives.

The font issue is one that touches every facet of working with legacy data. For that reason we will keep coming back to it. At this time, begin looking at the fonts used in your data to determine if you are going to encounter any of the following problems:

- **Custom fonts:** These may have been designed in-house using a font tool or purchased from a vendor. Custom fonts may look like other fonts but contain alternative mappings or additional, non-standard characters. It is important to find out as much as you can about any custom fonts in use.

- **Corporate identity fonts:** These may be standard font families, such a Garamond, Gill Sans, or even Times, but they have special meaning because they are used to define corporate branding elements. If there is a corporate font, find out who is responsible for it ,and find out how much room they will give you when you are moving corporate documents to new environments.

- **Platform-dependent or vendor-specific fonts:** These are fonts that are designed for a specific print or other output device. Fonts delivered with IBM printers, such as GT10 and the Sonoran family, or for the Xerox printers, such as PR111E or P0612B are platform-dependent fonts that will require special care during a migration.

- **Resolution-specific fonts:** These are fonts designed for printing at a specific resolution. Original IBM AFP printers have fonts that were designed for printing at approximately 240 dots-per-inch. Most Xerox devices of the same era print at 300 dots-per-inch. Developing web-friendly alternatives that exactly match fonts developed for these resolutions is not always possible.

- **Symbol fonts:** Every print manufacturer recognized the need for special symbols. Each approached the requirement differently, leaving us with many incompatible methods for getting industry-specific symbols into print files. As you analyze print output, keep an eye open to symbols that are not part of standard font sets and be sure that you learn how they are inserted into the print file.

Now let us look at some of the same types of issues with regard to the graphic elements of the print files. For each graphic you will need to know:

- **Bitmap or Vector:** Most graphics are bitmap graphics, which means that if you open the file the image is represented as strings of dots that form the image. Vector graphics use print formulas to cause the image to be drawn.

- **Resolution:** What is the resolution of the bitmap graphic format generally in use? This is usually the same as the resolution of the printer in use, but not always. In some situations graphics may reside in files at one resolution and print at some other resolution. Especially in environments where there are AFP and Xerox printers in use you should verify how the bitmap graphics are created and stored.

- **Color:** Most graphics will be stored as pure black and white or as gray-scale graphics. There have been spot color printers and full color printers available for some years, however, and if your company is an early adopter of technology, find out if there are production graphics that contain color information.

- **Graphic Applications:** What created the original graphics? Be prepared for a long list of applications residing on multiple platforms. It is common to find that there are graphic programs on the host, midrange, and network platforms, all contributing files for use in the production print environment.

For each application you approach, you must decide if it is important for *your* documents to maintain their fidelity to the print version. That means not only looking identical to the paper in terms of the font and format. You will have to look at characters sets, line spacing, and inter-character spacing. Some legacy applications were created using tools that permitted the document creator a lot of flexibility in the formatting.

You may discover that line spacing was compressed, inter-character spacing was condensed or expanded, and even individual pairs of characters had spacing altered to meet the needs of the document owner (it's called kerning). Some of these characteristics may not survive a migration to a new output environment.

Kerning

In the following example the first A and W are in their natural positions. The second and third pairs have been kerned to make them easier to read.

AW   Natural

AW   Metric Kerning

AW   Optical Kerning

Continuing the Evaluation

The evaluation continues with a look at those lists we started at the beginning of the project. You should have a good idea of the breadth of your document library, with a special appreciation for the following issues:

- The documents/files you create,

- Which documents are intended to be migrated to new output environments,

- Which documents are likely to pose the *largest* problems,

- Which documents are likely to pose the *smallest* problems.

If you are not yet sure, go back to your lists and review them carefully. Look for ways to classify documents by type and by the resources they use. Single out those files that appear to use unusual fonts. Which documents rely on a print post-processor to generate the print? Remember that many of your simple line data print jobs rely on complex job management scripts (JCL Print PROCs, page definitions and form definitions in AFP; JDLs and DJDEs in Xerox print).

Control Files

- Datastream/vendor specific
- Define physical and logical printer characteristics to the datastream, including page dimensions and resource locations
- **AFP:** PageDef and FormDef
- **Xerox:** JDE, JSL, PDE, CME
- May be embedded/inline or external
- Provide setup information that is vital to the printer, and therefore the transform program
- If they are mismatched to the file to be transformed, the result is unpredictable and generally undesirable.

You should now be able to identify what you have so that you can categorize the characteristics of the documents and other program output. From this point forward we are going to concentrate on the issues involved in moving to a web-enabled platform, but the rules and requirements apply to most of the new devices you might want to add to your environment. Whether it's a WAP-enabled cell phone or Bluetooth™ wireless handheld, the rules will remain the same.

Migration Point

There are many stops between the data and the final output. The challenge in moving or re-purposing that final output is in acquiring all of the same resources the print engine had available when the print was generated. There are three paths you can use to acquire the print data.

Acquire it:

- During document generation

- After document generation

- After print file generation

Creating an alternative version of a document during the document generation process means that the application must be capable of producing two files. Some applications can do this with a simple addition of a parameter, while other applications can only produce a single stream per execution of the application. In many respects, this is the optimum way to create two alternative output streams because the source data should be identical while the output parameters can be tuned for each environment.

For example, imagine an application that can produce the AFP needed to print 8.5" x 11" pages in portrait orientation, while at the same time producing a PDF file for web viewing using standard screen output parameters. The users of the print document have what they need, while the users of the screen-viewing version have a more appropriate look and feel to their version of the document.

Very few older applications can use this approach, however. For most applications the final version of the document, with all of the variables fully resolved, is not available until the document is generated. When this is the situation, look at post-processing solutions to move the data to a viewing environment.

You'll see this when you use products that replace fields and placeholders in the document with variable data from an outside source to create a final document. Mail merging programs and even programs that assemble user manuals and insurance policies from libraries of possible paragraph and chapter combinations fall into this category. Until that process is complete, there isn't a document ready to move to a new environment.

The same is true if the complete document is not available until the end of the print process, though the process of getting to a web version gets a bit more complicated. If the document is completed on the way to the printer, and does not normally reside on a hard drive on any system before printing, the trick will be to capture the print stream on the way to the printer to create something that can be migrated.

As you look at the projects that are candidates for migration, try to start with the simpler documents to work out the problems. It is not a good idea to tackle a document that has variable data replacement issues on top of transformation issues as the first project.

Begin by identifying formatting issues that may cause problems. These include:

- Proprietary file formats for fonts and graphics
- Color in the print stream
- External formatting applied to data files
- External resources and transforms

None of these problems is insurmountable, but knowing about the issues ahead of the migration is imperative.

The next area you should review is the formatting of the document. What kind of paper is the document intended to use? Letter, legal, A4, or A5? There are other choices, too. It might be a custom paper size with dye cuts or glue folds that required special formatting. Whatever the intended paper stock, the proportions for the output vary by size and page orientation. This may change the usability of the documents you want to move.

When you are moving documents, remember that large document output systems often have a number of post-processing steps. A common step is one that prepares the documents for binding. It is often called imposition, and you can think of it as a shuffling program that re-organizes the pages so that when they are printed they can be bound in the center for final delivery. A variation on an imposition program is one that tumbles every other page so that it prints upside-down on the reverse side of each page. This is common in legal and financial environments for documents that are bound at the top. For the purposes of the migration, you will usually want to capture the documents before such post-processing.

So, business printing has evolved to include a variety of proprietary formats and open standards. You don't need to become an expert in all of the print file formats, but it is easier to make good decisions if you understand the basic construction of the data formats you may encounter. We are going to look again at each of these formats.

- Line data
- AFP
- Xerox LCDS/Metacode
- Xerox UDK/XES
- PostScript/PDF
- HP PCL

Each of the datastreams has challenges and opportunities associated with it, which we will note along the way. It is not possible to do a comprehensive job on each datastream, though. If you need more information check the appendices for references to available manuals and companies that can help.

Line Data and Line Printers 101

Round 5

Since line data forms the bulk of the printing done around the world, understanding it is important. In this section we look at the various forms of line data and where the problem areas are.

Line Data: ASCII or EBCDIC

Documents: What are they and who owns them?

Conditioning: What do you do to format the data?

Expect a few surprises along the way!

Line data is the most basic and the most difficult form of data to work with. The most common form of line data is created on an IBM mainframe (or IBM-compatible mainframe) using EBCDIC encoding. In most corporate print shops the line data is a record and column-oriented print line format based on the development of print output for IBM 3211 and 1403 impact line printers, and printers that emulated them. Another possibility is that your line data originates on a mid-range system or network where the encoding is in ASCII. Often ASCII line data emulates IBM network printers, such as the IBM ProPrinter.

This is an important point because the line data that originates on IBM mainframes and their equivalents is usually record and column oriented. That means that there are lines of data are sensitive to what data is in what position on the line within the record and that at the end of each line, or record, there is often some kind of end-of-record marker. When line data originates in a network or mid-range environment it is more common for the data to be generated as a *stream* of data, not the records or lines of data in the host environment.

It will be important for you to know where your line data originates because in some environments, to make the network and host data work together, programmers added post-processing steps to condition the data so it would work together. If you have one of those environments, you will need to know where this conditioning takes place.

If it were just a matter of which encoding scheme is in use, working with line data would be easy. Unfortunately, there are also a variety of coding schemes inside the data records that are used to format and otherwise alter the appearance of the data.

Line data that originates on a mainframe usually contains carriage controls. Carriage controls are exactly what they sound like. They originally controlled the print head on the impact printers, giving print programmers the ability to overstrike characters to create bold text, underscore text by making a second pass with an underscore character, strike out text by over-striking, or alter the inter-line spacing by adding carriage returns.

Sounds simple, until we add that carriage controls come in either machine carriage control or ANSI carriage control, depending on the nature of the original impact device the line data was designed for.

Carriage controls precede the data on the line to indicate how it should be handled. Many print programs rely on the carriage controls, which is why it is important to know what kind of carriage controls are in the data.

While you are looking at carriage controls, there may also be Table Reference Characters (TRCs) or Font Index Bytes

ANSI Carriage Control

All ANSI carriage controls print after spacing. The codes may be in EBCDIC or ASCII.

+	Space zero lines - overprint.
<space>	Space one line.
0	Space two lines.
-	Space three lines.
1-9,	Skip to channels 1-9.
A-C,	Skip to channels 10, 11 and 12.

Machine Carriage Control (IBM1403)

0x03 - comment. Do not print or space

Below codes do not print the data on the record, only space...

0x0b - space 1
0x13 - space 2

0x1b - space 3

Below codes do not print data, but skip to a specific channel or column of data.

0x83 - skip to channel 0
0x8b - skip to channel 1
0x93 - skip to channel 2
0x9b - skip to channel 3
0xa3 - skip to channel 4
0xab - skip to channel 5
0xb3 - skip to channel 6
0xbb - skip to channel 7
0xc3 - skip to channel 8
0xcb - skip to channel 9
0xd3 - skip to channel 10
0xdb - skip to channel 11
0xe3 - skip to channel 12

Below codes print before spacing...

0x01 - space 0. just print
0x09 - space 1
0x11 - space 2
0x19 - space 3

Below codes print before skipping to a channel.

0x89 - print and skip to channel 1
0x91 - print and skip to channel 2
0x99 - print and skip to channel 3
0xa1 - print and skip to channel 4
0xa9 - print and skip to channel 5
0xb1 - print and skip to channel 6
0xb9 - print and skip to channel 7
0xc1 - print and skip to channel 8
0xc9 - print and skip to channel 9
0xd1 - print and skip to channel 10
0xd9 - print and skip to channel 11
0xe1 - print and skip to channel 12

(FIBs) between the carriage control byte and the start of the data. These tell the print program to use a specific font for the line of data. TRCs and FIBs don't give a font name, however, only a font position in a predefined set of fonts allocated to the printer.

In some cases you will find mainframe-generated line data that does not contain carriage controls or any other control bytes preceding the data. This situation usually means that the data was generated for use with a specific type of application program. It may be that every record is the exact same record length (LRECL), which is referred to as a fixed length record: the application knows the record length and begins reading a new record when a fixed number of bytes are processed.

There may be line feed (LF) characters at the end of the data record, or you may find a combination carriage return/ line feed (CRLF) at the end of the record. It all depends on how the line data was styled to work with the target applications.

It will be imperative to know what you have and how the data responds to the current formatting so that you can make the best decisions about setting up new output environments.

For example, if a line data application produces data that is 132 bytes/characters wide and 24 lines deep on each page, using a font that formats at 12 characters to the inch, you know that your output is normally 11 inches wide. By re-mapping the font to a view-friendly size, it may be possible to display the data without making any additional changes and without forcing the reader to scroll left and right. This is the type of information you need to derive about how the print output is generated.

You may also find that, as a condition for using a commercial application program or even to aide the development of an in-house business system, it was necessary to condition the line data. It is common to find coding of additional prefixes and suffixes to the data records for use by these programs. For example, a character in the third byte of every line of a data may indicate if there is an additional document to be added to the package, or a trailing byte on the data record might indicate the end of a document and cause the output to jog left or right in the output bin. All of these things are important as you look to re-direct the output.

You might also find the use of meaningful comments to alter the nature of the document, cause insertion of variable data into the output, or any number of other processing options. The use of the comment records became popular during the 1980s and 1990s, especially by commercial applications. Often the comment records have a specified structure used by a post-processing module.

If you discover that significant processing occurs as the result of prefix bytes, suffix bytes, or comment records, the job of getting the data to the Web generally requires the use of a datastream transform that runs after the final application processing is complete.

Line data may also contain space characters to create a formatted look to the data. Those spaces exist as real hex values in the data that will exist in any new output environment, where they may no longer be appropriate. The same is true of underlines placed in the text using carriage controls to cause over-striking, or bold text caused by over-striking. These are just a few more of the challenges.

The most important thing to remember about line data is that you are dealing with a form that relies on records of data. Each record has characteristics and the formatting of that record is based on the information contained in the record or modified by a control record. In your environment, you may have IBM formatting controls or Xerox formatting controls in addition to the carriage control records we mentioned a moment ago.

In an IBM line data environment, you may have files called page definitions, or PageDefs, and form definitions, or FormDefs, which allow the print programmer to manipulate the line data. These files usually reside on the host computer. They may add font information, conditionally remove some of the data or conditionally add more information to the print stream. These are extremely powerful controls, so if you are using them, you will need to learn how many of these PageDefs and FormDefs you use and what their functions are. We'll talk more about them in the next chapter.

If you are in a Xerox line data environment, you have the same challenge. Instead of PageDef and FormDef files, you have DJDEs, JDE, JDLs, PDEs and CMEs, among other resources. These resource descriptors interpret the line data on the way to the printer, and can not only add fonts, add graphics, and add form overlays, but they can reposition the output data. In addition, because this all usually happens on the printer, when you take the printer out of the mix you can run into a few challenges. We'll talk more about these resources in the next chapter, as well.

All Points Addressability: IBM & Xerox

Round 6

While line data is the majority of the print data in the world today, there are large applications in banking, finance and insurance designed for high-speed All Points Addressable printers. In this section we are going to look at each of the datastreams more closely to identify the challenges.

APA Datastreams: AFP, Metacode, PostScript, PCL, and PDF

APA Resources: PageDefs, FormDefs, DJDEs, JDEs, JDLs, CMEs, PDEs, Fonts, Forms, Graphics

Pay close attention to the history of the datastreams. It may help you diagnose anomalies in your output during testing.

Unlike line data, *all points addressability* in a print datastream requires information encoded about the data, its formatting resources, and its target environment. Moving beyond formatting based on where a character is relative to the beginning of a data record requires a more robust method of identifying the components of the print data, including the ability to manipulate the incoming data by stripping characters, adding formatting, and redirecting formatting.

IBM and Xerox developed *all points addressable* (APA) printers in response to their customers. Insurance companies, banks, and other organizations whose primary product requires extensive paper back up, wanted to take the level of their print up another notch. While they could produce paper at high speeds in the line printer world, and control some of the look of their printed output with pre-printed forms and color stock, they really wanted a typeset look and feel to all of their communication with their customers. And, the more customization they could add, the better.

With all points addressable technology almost any point on the page could be addressed with a spot of toner. We say almost because each printer has areas on a page that can't be reached. The quality of the print becomes a function of the number of spots of toner (sometimes called dots or pels) the printer could place. Of course, the more dots per inch the printer has to control, the more data there is travelling across the network and to the printer. Each vendor came up with their own solutions to that issue. IBM's original APA solution produced print at 240 dpi, while Xerox's original APA solution produced print at 300 dpi.

IBM responded with their Advanced Function Presentation (AFP) architecture and a range of printers to support it. They encouraged participation in the architecture by making it open and documented. Xerox, however, did not participate and went their own way with their high-speed Metacode/LCDS printers.

The desktop printer manufacturers were also moving away from dot matrix printers and daisy wheel printers, toward new technologies like lasers and ink jet. Hewlett Packard's LaserJets, DeskJets, and other inkjet printers began to appear in office environments, fulfilling the need for short run convenience printing from the ever-expanding world of network-based business computing. Joining HP were a variety of PostScript printer vendors producing very high quality output.

IBM's AFP and the Xerox print environments dominated print output during the 1980s and most of the 1990s. In the mid-1990s the infusion of print hardware offerings with departmental devices that offered midrange PCL and PostScript printing began to change the landscape and push application vendors to support the formerly desktop-only print formats from host-based applications. Both formats have been working their way onto the higher-speed print devices ever since, blurring the older distinction we used to make between high-speed centralized print devices managed by the IT department and the departmental and desktop devices. For today, most of you have AFP and/or Xerox environments to manage, so we will start here.

All points addressability technology brings a more sophisticated look to a document, but it also brings more weight to the print environment. AFP and Xerox print streams owned the corporate print environments because you could manage the print files within the confines of available bandwidth between the host and the printer, and the available disk space. With the largest print jobs, even the most efficient print environments are not enough, however. In large enterprise print shops a job could spool to the print queue for hours and then take hours more to print. As important as the look of the documents is as a tool for corporate communication, the realities of hardware constraints and available print windows often played a part in what could be printed.

This is changing as the processors on mainframes and networks become faster, bandwidths for inter-device communication expand, and even spool storage methodologies are enhanced. Over time expect to see PostScript and PDF jobs becoming more common in enterprise printing. Internal and external customers continue to demand more sophisticated documents, and while AFP and the Xerox formats continue to grow to handle color and higher resolution, PostScript and PDF may win the battle over time since it is a mature technology with a wide range of output environments at the high-end and the low-end of the print speed range.

AFP Ramp-Up

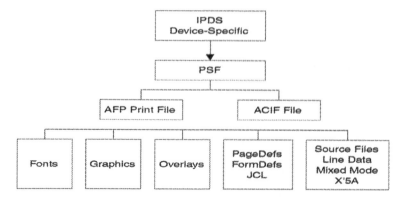

We often talk about the world of high-speed, enterprise printing as being in one of two camps: IBM or Xerox. They are really only two of the many print device vendors that supply the corporate printing market. If you check carefully, you find that when most people discuss their IBM printer, they are really talking about AFP printing. The actual print device may have been sold by a number of other print vendors, including Lexmark, Océ Printing Systems, MPI/i-data, LSI Intermate, or even Xerox.

IBM defined and promoted Advanced Function Printing/ Presentation (AFP) as an open architecture for information delivery. While the original emphasis was getting toner on sheets of paper using all points addressable (APA) technology, over time it evolved to include information delivery to any platform. IBM encouraged adoption by other print device vendors, by application software companies, and end users by inviting participation in the on-going definition and direction of the architecture.

One of the design goals behind the AFP architecture was to create a way to define the print data so that it could remain independent of the final output device, much like PostScript. It had to be versatile enough to handle the legacy data of the line printers, but robust enough to handle the requirements of placing a dot of toner anywhere on a sheet of paper or turn on a pixel anywhere on viewing device. In addition, the architecture had to be defined in such a way that third party application vendors as well as

MO:DCA & OCA'S

- MO:DCA: Mixed Object: Document Content Architecture
- PTOCA (presentation text/lines)
- IOCA (image)
- GOCA (vector graphics)
- BCOCA (bar codes)
- FOCA (fonts)

Watch for multimedia objects to handle audio, video and application launchers

in-house development teams could develop output modules that produced AFP datastreams.

While creating a printer-independent architecture is a significant challenge, it was only part of the requirement. It was still necessary to create files that would print on the many print devices sold and supported by IBM, as well as a number of other vendors. AFP succeeded by defining and architecture that allowed for line data, while also defining structured fields to control the information contained in the print datastream. There are structures for handling graphics, fonts, electronic forms overlays, and even the variations in line data.

AFP print environments handle both older line data and AFP structured print data under the umbrella of MO:DCA (Mixed Object: Document Content Architecture). The architecture permits mixed-mode print files containing line data and AFP structures, as well as packaged AFP created by programs like IBM's AFP Conversion and Indexing Facility (ACIF). The MO:DCA architecture also supports non-MO:DCA structures, including PDF, TIFF, and Encapsulated PostScript (EPS). However, AFP is not usually what you print.

The printer-specific portion of the architecture is the Intelligent Printer Data Stream, or IPDS. Each output device has its own variation of IPDS to allow the print data to use the print device to its best advantage. The original

Inside a 5A Record:
This is a Begin Active Environment Group

CHAR   1 LyI 1

ZONE   501DAC000F4444444

NUMR   A0038900110000000

           01...5...10...15..

bridge program between the device independent AFP and the device dependent IPDS is the Print Services Facility, or PSF.

PSF and the components of the AFP architecture worked together to ensure that most jobs that printed on IBM equipment could make the transition to the new world of high-speed laser printers without changing the original applications. AFP environments usually rely on the software services residing on the host or network rather than acting as standalone devices, as is often found in Xerox printing environments, so it could print EBCDIC line data when attached to IBM hosts and also handle ASCII line data when attached to UNIX (including IBM's AIX) and LAN environments.

When you work with AFP data, it is important to remember that most AFP print files contain only a small portion of the information necessary to generate the final print or view image. There may be many external resources mapped to the print environment. In most print shops the resource files containing fonts, graphics, and the control files reside in PSF libraries. In many IT environments there are dedicated PSF libraries for each application, while in others a PSF production library is maintained for use by all production print jobs, with additional libraries defined for testing and development.

One more caveat. The ACIF program we mentioned a

moment ago can be a great help or a major problem, depending on how it was configured in your environment.

ACIF was designed to package AFP print jobs so that they contained all of the resources needed to reproduce the job. It was originally conceived as a way to build packages of AFP for archiving, so it has options that allow you to add indexing information. In its original application, it proved to be more of a problem, though, when working with runs of tens of thousands of pages of data. That meant the addition of configuration parameters that allowed a programmer to specify which resources would be packaged in the AFP file and which would not. In many environments the common resources, like logos, are never included in the ACIF AFP package.

So, if you know that you run ACIF in your environment, you should check with the programmers who build the configuration files to learn what is included in the AFP package and what is not.

What are AFP Resources?

We use the term resources to encompass all of the files that must be available to the print job and PSF to accomplish the final print or view. In an AFP printing environment you might have any or all of the following resource types:

- PageDefs
- FormDefs
- Fonts/Codepages
- Page Segments
- Electronic Overlays

Each of the resources provides information about the print job. The PageDef defines the physical page in terms of its orientation and dimensions. The FormDef defines the logical page as it relates to the physical page. Fonts define the look of the text on the page, and page segments provide graphics. Overlays provide pre-printed text, usually acting as a replacement for pre-printed form stock.

Page Definitions

- Specify AFP options for line data
- Number of print lines per page
- Page orientation & dimensions
- Page ejects
- Uses *page formats*, AKA *data maps*, to vary formatting by page
- Conditional and field processing
- Overlays
- Start with D3A8CB triplet
- End with D3A9CB triplet

A PageDef resource defines the size and print direction of the logical page. When used with line data it provides the font list accessed by TRC bytes in the data and processes the carriage control bytes to imitate the formatting of the line data.

A PageDef can also be used to manipulate the incoming data by applying conditional processing options. For example, options can be established that cause page breaks based on the number of print lines per page or even trigger strings in the incoming text. It is possible to specify new formatting options and to add variable data attributes that control the positioning of text blocks, apply fonts, repeat or omit data strings and insert constant text strings.

PageDefs use internal objects called page formats or data maps to process and manipulate the incoming data on a page basis. They are created as source files and compiled into the object file used by PSF. One of the advantages of AFP printings is that a PageDef can have many page formats defined to allow pages with different characteristics to be handled as a part of the same job.

PAGEDEF Example

```
PAGEDEF OUT1
    WIDTH 297 MM   HEIGHT 210 MM
    DIRECTION ACROSS
    REPLACE YES ;
  FONT FONT0 CS H200 CP V10500 HEIGHT  16;
  FONT FONT1 544063  HEIGHT  72 RATIO 200 ;
  FONT FONT2 544063 HEIGHT 36;
PRINTLINE
    CHANNEL 1
    POSITION  0 IN 0 IN  ;
  FIELD START  1  LENGTH  2
       POSITION  1.0 IN  1.0 IN
       FONT FONT0 ;
  FIELD START  3  LENGTH  2
       POSITION  1.0 IN  3.0 IN
       FONT FONT1 ;
  FIELD START  5  LENGTH  2
       POSITION  1.0 IN  3.0 IN
       FONT FONT2 ;
```

Form Definitions

- Define printer-specific and printing-specific parameters:
  - Offset with respect to media
  - Power Positioning (multi-up or n-up)
  - Duplex/Simplex
  - Include Overlay
  - Field suppression
- Uses *copy groups*, AKA *media maps*, to vary formatting by copy
- Start with D3A8CD triplet
- End with D3A9CD triplet

FormDefs define the printer-specific and printing-specific parameters of the print job. It controls the offset of the print image with respect to the paper as well as options like simplex (single side) or duplex (two-sided) printing. Enhancements to the AFP environment over the years added the ability to use FormDefs to invoke multi-up printing, where multiple logical pages are printed on a single physical page to conserve paper.

FORMDEF Sample

```
FORMDEF  A10110
     REPLACE YES;
     COPYGROUP F1A10110
          DUPLEX NO
          BIN 1
          JOG NO
          OFFSET .165 IN .165 IN
          ADJUST 0
          SUBGROUP    COPIES 1
               FLASH NO
     COPYGROUP F1A1011B
          DUPLEX YES
          BIN 2
          JOG YES
```

FormDefs use copy groups, also called media maps, to vary formatting, including the inclusion or substitution of electronic overlays, suppression of incoming data fields, and even print control such as direction of the output to specific bins. Like PageDefs, they are created in a source format and compiled into the object format used by PSF.

Fonts, Graphics and Overlays

Fonts, graphics and overlays are covered in depth in later chapters, but we will start by setting the baseline here.

Starting with fonts, remember that font files are licensed

from the vendor. In fact, they are subject to the same licensing restrictions as any software program you purchase. In most AFP environments there is a starter set of fonts that came as part of the PSF package, often called the PSF Compatibility font set. The fonts in this set were designed to provide backward compatibility with earlier print environments, including impact printers.

To provide more attractive formatting alternatives IBM also sold the Sonoran Serif and Sonoran Sans Serif font sets for use on their 240 dpi laser printers. These fonts roughly emulated the Times New Roman and Helvetica typefaces, but were massaged for better results in the 240 dpi print environment.

When you plan your migration remember that these fonts were developed prior to the development of the Internet and the web. Finding compatible fonts that work consistently in a viewing environment is often a challenge.

To make matters worse, IBM made several font utilities available, including the Font Library Services Facility (FLSF), Type Transformer, and FontLab, that permitted a user to wreak havoc on a font. Many found that commercial products like Fontgrapher and FontMonger could be used to modify character rasters and add new characters to a font, too. We'll talk more about fonts later.

You might hear the terms unbounded box fonts and bounded box fonts as you are doing your preliminary investigation. Unbounded box fonts are the older font technology usually associated with the IBM 3800 printers, where character positioning and orientation was defined within the raster pattern for each character. These fonts were encoded to print at a specific orientation, usually portrait or landscape.

Bounded box fonts were the next technology in fonts. It came along with the introduction of the IBM 3820 printers. In bounded box fonts the character positioning is external to the raster pattern, meaning that only one font was required regardless of the page print orientation, though fonts were still stored as a combination of character set (the raster images of the characters) and codepage (the mapping

AFP Font Variations

- Unbounded Box Fonts: IBM 3800; character positioning and orientation within the raster pattern
- Bounded Box: IBM 3820; character positioning is external to the raster pattern
- Outline Fonts: Vector form of fonts; scalable
- DBCS (Double Byte Character Set) is used in Asia Pacific (Japan, Korea, Taiwan, China, Hong Kong).

of the raster images to the hex values for the characters), and the mapping file.

Double byte character sets (DBCS) handle fonts for most Asian countries where the standard encoding schemes do not support enough variation. If you have documents that use DBCS characters sets and plan to migrate to PDF or HTML, you should be successful since there fonts available, but plan on testing diligently.

Font technology has continued to evolve to include scalable outline fonts, originally found in the desktop publishing domain. Outline fonts are stored in a vector format, which allows them to be scaled to precise increments by the software.

Page Segments

Page segments in the AFP print environment refer to the graphics, usually raster image files, placed in the print stream. They may be inline in the AFP data or called using a reference to an external file. Older AFP page segments usually contain resolution dependent image data, called IM1, that cannot be scaled, clipped, cropped, or rotated in the AFP datastream. This is an important point for shops with several types of AFP print devices because you may find libraries of graphics with identical names but stored at different resolutions. Newer Page Segments can contain scalable graphics in some environments, so part of the investigation includes determining which types of graphics you have and where they are used.

In the early days of AFP, the graphics were usually created on a host machine using an IBM tool like the Graphical Data Display Manager (GDDM). Some of those GDDM-based programs are still in use alongside user-written programs and third-party application graphic tools tied into applications that provided the data to pie charts and bar graphs.

As AFP evolved, the support for AFP graphics migrated down to the desktop, with support for page segment creation emerging in a number of graphic software packages. A number of transform programs also emerged to convert graphics created on a PC to the page segment format so that they could be uploaded to PSF libraries and used in AFP printing. We'll look at the details of AFP graphics in a later chapter.

Overlays

The electronic forms used in place of pre-printed forms are called *overlays*. IBM introduced the Overlay Generation Language (OGL) as the tool of choice to create overlays, although over time it was often replaced by more familiar desktop word processing packages working in conjunction with the AFP Workbench. Products from Elixir Technologies, ISIS, Lytrod, and others also supported the creation of overlays on the desktop for use in AFP printing from any platform.

Electronic forms are used to provide the static boilerplate information common to many business print applications. The boilerplate information may contain text, image data, and graphics, and even complex drawings using circles, paths and shading. The overlays are used in an object form, either compiled from OGL source or provided by third party

AFP Page Origin

Upper left corner of the presentation space.

X: From Origin, increases across the top of the medium
   If portrait, across short edge;
   if landscape, across long edge

Y: From Origin, increases down the side of the medium
   If portrait, down the long edge;
   if landscape down the short edge

applications. Those objects may be included inline in the print stream or called by reference from an external library.

There used to be a limit of eight overlays per physical page in most AFP environments, though that increased to 254 overlays in later releases. That poses a few considerations. If you are working in an AFP environment that has not had a software upgrade in many years, you may still have the limit of eight overlays per page. And, if you still have that limit you may have had some creative print programmers who found ways to program around the limit. That kind of creative programming can cause problems as you try to re-purpose your content.

Even if you have upgraded to the most recent support in your AFP environment, you may find that there are still applications using old routines that manipulate overlays in groups of eight. Again, the point is to be aware of the possibilities so you can handle them gracefully during your migration, transform, or re-purpose tasks. It is also an issue as you begin your testing of the new output. Make sure that you know what overlays are expected so that you can compare the new output to the original to verify that all of the overlays are still present.

AFP Printing

In most AFP printing environments, Print Services Facility (PSF) software or a PSF look-alike (like Oce Prisma, which used to be called PS8000) converts AFP to IPDS for printing. We mentioned earlier that IPDS is the device-specific form of the print datastream. IPDS devices are often considered to be 240 dpi, 300 dpi and 600 dpi devices, though internally the AFP world now processes at 14400 units per inch.

These printers may support highlight color or four-color printing depending on the device and its configuration. In addition to the variations in resolution and color support, IPDS printers have different *unprintable areas* depending on the model and manufacturer. The unprintable area is where the print head cannot place toner or ink. The variations between printers happen because of the different printer designs and different print head designs. You'll see a big difference between the unprintable areas on printers designed to be roll fed versus those designed to be sheet feed.

Jobs designed to print on more than one AFP device generally approach the issue of margins conservatively, defining documents so that they will print on the device with the smallest printable area. When migrating these jobs to new print environments it is still possible to encounter difficulty with the density of the text in relation to the printable area, but when moving to viewing environments this problem often disappears.

AFP printing is supported by IBM, Lexmark, Océ, Xerox, MPI/I-data, and many others, as direct printer manufacturers or through the use of conversion boxes that handle incoming IPDS streams designed for specific printers. Find out how many manufacturers boxes you have in your environment and what applications print to them as part of your inventory and assessment.

Xerox Ramp-up

When we talk about printing in the IBM environment we generally concentrate on their AFP print format, although many IBM printers will now handle PostScript and PDF. In the Xerox environment we have much more to consider. Xerox sells printers that can handle just about any file format you might want to print, including line data and AFP. Not every printer can handle every format, but something in the product line is likely to handle what you need.

Over the past 20 years, Xerox has sold printers in all of the following groups:

- High-speed centralized production printers/ Print Language: Metacode/DJDE
- High-speed production printers/ Print Language: PostScript
- Medium-speed departmental printers/ Print Languages: PCL, PS, IPDS
- Low-speed departmental printers/ Print Languages: XES/UDK, PostScript

The product line is versatile, but they all speak different languages and many speak more than one. That means that

Basic Metacodes

X'00' Font Selection
X'01' Record End
X'02' Select Landscape
X'03' Overstrike
X'04' Absolute Y (Dot) Position
X'05' Relative Y (Dot) Position
X'06' Absolute X (Scan) Position
X'07' Relative X (Scan) Position
X'08' Modify Character
X'09' Select Portrait

Conditioned Line Data: DJDE

Describes line data with embedded command records to
set fonts, and call graphics, forms, and logos

Interleaves line data structures with resources using
DJDEs - the command records

DJDEs are human-readable commands that are
interpreted in real-time during the print job

DJDE records begin with a DJDE Identifier, a string
that tells the printer to interpret what follows as
DJDE commands. Common DJDE IDENs are $$Xerox and
$$DJDE

simply identifying the printer as a *Xerox printer* is not
enough information. To make intelligent decisions you have
to know much more.

Even if you look at just the Xerox centralized production
printers, you find a variety of possible print languages and
file formats. There is no architecture behind the print file
format, as in the AFP world. A Xerox customer may be
printing in a variety of formats on the same physical device,
including:

- Metacode
- Metacode and line data conditioned with DJDEs
- Line data conditioned with control files (JDL/JDE)
- Line data with embedded DJDE statements

Metacode is the native, low-level language of the Xerox
family of centralized high-speed printers. The *metacodes* are
hex values that invoke printer actions, such as moving the
print head to a specific position on the paper, or switching a
font. They are analogous to the escape sequences in PCL or
XES/UDK printing, but built for efficiency and print speed.

If you open a Metacode file with an ASCII text editor, you see hex values, the metacodes. They are interspersed with print data and, often, additional printer control commands: the DJDEs. To make it more confusing, a Xerox Metacode printer can switch between ASCII and EBCDIC within the same print job.

In addition to print files that use the metacodes, the Xerox Metacode printer supports line data files, conditioned with compiled job control files, embedded DJDEs, or both. The majority of all printing on Xerox systems is line data conditioned with DJDEs.

Xerox also supports mixed-mode printing. When Xerox print files are in mixed mode, some printing characteristics are set with metacodes, while others are set with Dynamic Job Descriptor Entries (DJDEs), the subset of the Job Description Language (JDL) used to create compiled job control files. DJDE commands, which are interpreted directly by the printer, may change a font, call a new electronic form, cause a page eject, or start a new job. Mixed mode jobs are sometimes the output of programs created by application vendors.

All of the information about how a print job is constructed and how it should behave on the printer is managed in the print environment description defined in the Job Descriptor Entries (JDEs). Any print job may invoke any number of JDEs during a print job, providing incredible flexibility.

Where Metacode and the compiled print objects are not generally readable, DJDEs are easily identified in print files as a series of parameters and attributes following a DJDE Identifier.

Providing even more flexibility are the attachment options. These printers may be attached as an *online* device to a mainframe host or to a network, or they may run *offline* attached to tape drives or server environments that behave like tape drives. This is important because the composition of the datastream is actually a bit different depending on how the print device acquires the data to print. Look at our JSL file example closely and you'll see different settings for online and offline.

JDL Example

```
MMMJDL: JDL;
VFU001: VFU      ASSIGN=(1,1),
            TOF=1,
            BOF=66;
PDFLT:  PDE      BEGIN=(1,.5),
            PMODE=LANDSCAPE,
            FONTS=(L0112B,9);
PDFLT1: PDE      BEGIN=(0,0),
            PMODE=PORTRAIT,
            FONTS=UN111E;
RPG:    TABLE    CONSTANT=(X'FFFF20FFFF');
RST:    TABLE    CONSTANT=(E'REPORT END');
RAX:    TABLE    CONSTANT=(X'111111111111111');
ROF:    TABLE    CONSTANT=(X'121212121212121212');
RPGONL: CRITERIA CONSTANT=(1,5,EQ,RPG);
RSTONL: CRITERIA CONSTANT=(0,10,EQ,RST);
ROFONL: CRITERIA CONSTANT=(0,8,EQ,ROF);
RPGOFF: CRITERIA CONSTANT=(2,5,EQ,RPG);
RSTOFF: CRITERIA CONSTANT=(1,10,EQ,RST);
ROFOFF: CRITERIA CONSTANT=(1,8,EQ,ROF);
        ACCT     USER=NONE;
MMONL: JDE;
        VOLUME   HOST=IBMONL, LABEL=NONE, CODE=NONE;
        IDEN     PREFIX='$MMDJ$',
            SKIP=10,
            OFFSET=1;
        RSTACK   TEST=RSTONL,
            DELIMITER=YES;
        RAUX     TEST=RAXONL;
        ROFFSET  TEST=ROFONL;
        RPAGE    TEST=(RPGONL), SIDE=(NUFRONT,NOFFSET),
            WHEN=BOTTOM;
        LINE     DATA=(0,150),
            VFU=VFU001,
            FCB=IGNORE,
            UCSB=IGNORE;
        OUTPUT   FORMAT=PDFLT1,
            COPIES=1,
            DUPLEX=YES,
            GRAPHICS=YES,
            STOCKS=STKDMG;
        MESSAGE  ITEXT='EXECUTING UNDER >>>>
JDL=MMMJDL,JDE=MMONL';
MMSTON: JDE;
        VOLUME   HOST=IBMONL, LABEL=NONE,
            CODE=EBCDIC;
        IDEN     PREFIX='$MMDJ$',
            SKIP=10,
            OFFSET=1;
        LINE     DATA=(0,150),
            VFU=VFU001,
            FCB=IGNORE,
            UCSB=IGNORE;
        OUTPUT   FORMAT=PDFLT,
            COPIES=1, DUPLEX=YES;
MESSAGE  ITEXT='EXECUTING UNDER >>>>
JDL=MMMJDL,JDE=MMSTON';
        END;
```

In most printing environments using the Xerox ESS line of printers, the resources (fonts, graphics, control files, electronic forms) are stored on the printer's hard drive. The names of the files are referenced in the print stream and acquired from the printer storage. Note that we said *most* printing environments. There are environments that include some of the resources inline in the data, and others that mix inline and printer-resident resources on the print jobs.

There are two important concerns. The first is that resources that are printer-resident *can be* different on every physical print device. Hold on to that thought because we will come back to it several times in this section and in the sections related to graphic and font resources.

The other issue is that there is not usually a product like the AFP Print Services Facility (PSF) acting as a buffer between the application print file and the printer. Unlike an AFP printing environment, which is normally automated, Xerox printing often requires an operator to attend the machine and respond to prompts on a display console. While there are resource management products from companies like Barr, Option Software, Solimar, Spur, and others on the market, they are often not configured to act as a comprehensive manager in the way the PSF controls the overall AFP print environment. They may not manage the resources that reside on the hard drives of printers, even if they manage the print jobs themselves.

Xerox Resources

The Xerox resource package includes all of the support files that contribute to handling the way the print will look. They include an alphabet soup of files that generally reside on the printer's hard drive, although the resources can also be carried in the print file as *inline resources*.

- JSL, JDL, JDE, PDE, CME, DJDE
- IMG
- FRM
- FNT, LGO

A Metacode Page

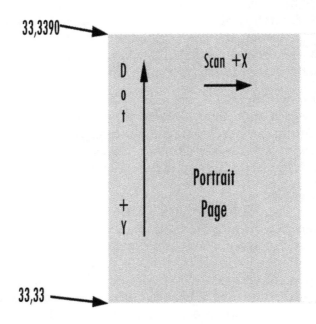

All of the resources listed in the first bullet relate to the job control information. JSL (Job Source Language) source files are compiled into JDL (Job Descriptor Language)/JDE (Job Descriptor Entry) files that define the physical and logical pages. The PDEs (Page Descriptor Entries) and CMEs (Copy Modification Entries) provide additional controls or resources, permitting conditional processing and alternative page handling.

The FNT (Font) files store the fonts in the Xerox proprietary format. Graphics may be stored in the IMG (Image) raster files, or in LGO (Logo) or FNT files as characters in a font. The only difference between an LGO file and an FNT file is that the LGO file carries within it the information needed to assemble the encoded characters into a graphic. This was a popular way to add graphic components to print jobs without encountering problems with memory and disk space limitations on the early Xerox printers. FRM files, originally created by Forms Description Language on the printer or on the mainframe using Host Forms Description Language (HFDL), store the electronic forms.

Most of the resources can be shared across the high-end printer line, although the unprintable areas do vary by model. Since Xerox did not originally provide an overall management scheme for managing the resources across the various devices, many environments discover that they have resources that share common names on multiple devices, but the information in the files is not identical. On the other hand, some environments go to great lengths to ensure that all of their devices share identical resources by acquiring third party packages like those we've mentioned, or developing complex load and backup procedures.

When plans to re-purpose, transform and migrate come into play, part of the challenge may come down to getting resources off of the printer. This often means second guessing information about the print jobs, including which physical printer they print on and what job (JDL) was really started on the printer. Even JDLs with the same name may have different characteristics on different printers.

Xerox Print Environment

The Metacode datastream makes use of special control words to pass information to the printer about environmental changes that need to be made, such as paper selection and offset stacking.

Four of the control words (RSTACK, ROFF, RPAGE, and RAUX) have no options and alter the printing environment merely by their presence. One other, the DJDE -- Dynamic Job Descriptor Entry -- we have mentioned previously, has many options, and is used to define printer resources, such as fonts and images, and page layout such as margins, positioning, and duplexing. The data sequence used to identify each control word is not defined by Xerox, but by you and your print programmers as part of the printer setup. Each control word must be defined as a series of hex values that start in a specified column and run for a given length. You can see this in the example of the JDL file in this section.

All of these values are defined as part of the printer setup. Although many companies use similar values, such as $$XEROX, $DJDE$, or $$DJDE for the DJDE, the actual values for these control words can vary from printer to printer, and from print job to print job.

The RSTACK command identifies the end of a print job. On most printers, once the RSTACK command is encountered, all printer values are returned to their default settings and the printer is returned line printer mode until another DJDE is encountered.

The ROFFSET command causes offset stacking. When an ROFFSET command is encountered, the next page will be offset stacked in the output tray. The RPAGE command selects which side of the page printing is to occur. The RAUX command causes paper to be selected from the auxiliary paper bin at the next page boundary.

This isn't every command, but they are the basics. Look at your operator manual for more variations and options, and talk to your print programmers to learn more about how they generally program.

The DJDE command selects printer resources, and defines page layout. In addition, it serves an unusual purpose in online IBM mainframe environments: selecting an ASCII datastream. The Metacode files shipped to the printer often have banner pages of some sort separating the print jobs. These banner pages are host-generated, and consist of simple EBCDIC characters, and carriage control. So that this information can be processed properly, the printer is initially in an EBCDIC line printer mode. It will stay in this EBCDIC mode until it encounters a DJDE in the datastream. Once the first DJDE has been processed, the printer will switch into an ASCII Metacode mode, and stay in that mode until the end of the job indicator, the RSTACK, is seen by the printer.

There are a few challenges resulting from this printing method:

- When host-attached, the first DJDE must be in EBCDIC, but following DJDE's must be in ASCII.

- Although the DJDE indicator itself may appear to be text (such as $$XEROX) it is actually only a series of hex values and should NOT be translated in any way, at any time.

- The occurrence of an RSTACK causes the printer to revert to EBCDIC line printer mode. Not all jobs are coded as they should be an often the RSTACK is missing.

The DJDE consists of the DJDE indicator, followed by one or more keywords that define printer options and resources. DJDEs usually come in packets of one or more records. Each record is ended by a semicolon, and the last record in the packet must be ended by the word END and a semicolon.

Here is a sample DJDE:

```
$$XEROX
JDL=MMMJDL,FONTS=(UN11OE,PO6BOB),DUPLEX=NO,;
$$XEROX JDE=MMONLI,FORMAT=MRM9,END;
```

The DJDE parameters are normally found in the back of the Operator's Manual for the printer. If you don't know where a copy is, locate one before you start your inventory. One of the items you need to keep track of is the DJDE indicator since it can vary by job and printer.

Xerox XES

While Xerox was penetrating the market with their high-end printers, they were also marketing a series of departmental printers that used a different print language. The Xerox Escape Sequence data stream, also known as UDK or User Defined Key, began by feeding the 2700 and

XES Example

```
=UDK=~
~+P,This is a sample form.
~+1Kosmos10-P
~+2Kosmos8-P
~+3YourSig24-P
~m660,34,30,90,400
~2~bMM Financial~p
888 Texas Street
Dallas, TX 76206
Attn: Testing Collector
~a1200,2580
~1Joanne C. Salt
~a1200,2533
1111 Dust Street
~a1200,2486
Dallas, TX 75206
Re: MasterCard No. 51234567891011121
~a500,2240
     BALANCE
~a500,2137
     AMOUNT DUE
~a900,2240
$
~a900,2137
$
~a984,2240
888.88
~a1012,2137
88.00
~a1200,2031
January 20, 2004
Dear Joanne C. Salt:
We appreciate your recent payment to your account,
however the amount was not sufficient to bring your balance
below your credit limit of $800.00.

Please curtail charges for the present and remit $ 88.00 to
overcome this situation.  We appreciate your patronage and
ask your cooperation in observing your credit limit.

A return envelope is enclosed. Please detach and return the
top portion of this letter with your payment or letter.

Sincerely,
~3ABCD   ç===== This is a callout to a signature font.
~1Testing Collector
214-555-1212
MM Financial
Dallas, TX 75206

51234567891011121
~+X
```

3700 series of printers, and later expanded to a wider range. While some companies used these printers to proof applications destined to run on their high-speed printers, most developed specific applications for the XES environment.

XES is an escape-driven file format that is used as both the application-generated print datastream that feeds the printer, and as a source file format for end users who choose to create the XES directly from a text editor. It relies on an escape sequence command, which is known to the printer, to direct text formatting. XES is so flexible that the user can set the escape command for every file they create. The escape command is also called the UDK, the key, and the XES command, so you might need to read through your documentation carefully to determine the escape sequence command identifier(s) used in your environment.

Remember, the escape command is not the ESCAPE key on your keyboard, but a character that acts as an identifier to the printer that what follows is a command instruction that must be interpreted, just as it is for PCL printers. Following the escape sequence command is the command instruction, which is case sensitive and which identifies the action to be taken by the printer on the data in the file.

In your XES file there are three kinds of XES commands: job control, simple formatting commands, and commands that can take variables. The job control XES commands set the job parameters, including the XES command symbol and the units of measure used in the job. It also sets printer-specific information like duplexing requirements.

The simple formatting commands are those like centering, flush left or right, and justification. Finally, the more common and more complex commands that use variables are those that set tabs, allow forms merging, set graphics in the file, and call fonts.

Because XES relies on hard record endings, you must take care when moving XES from one platform to another. If you lose the record endings, you have no way to identify the start of a new record. If you think that you have XES/UDK files that will be a part of your re-purposing and migration effort, locate as much information as you can about the applications, when they were written, and who maintains them today. These will be some of the toughest files to re-purpose.

Fonts in an XES file are accessed from the printer hard disk or included inline. Each character in an XES font is a bitmap/raster image at a specific point size, weight, resolution, and stress. This means that they are not scalable fonts.

Some files in an XES environment may not have a font command in them at all, instead relying on the default printer font to print the file. If there are font commands in the XES file, they are setup in stages. The first is the assignment of the font to a font ID, and then the calling of that ID with the appropriate font XES command. In the XES file the XES environment is established so that the printer knows what font to use and makes decisions about the white space between lines and characters based on the font metrics encoded in the font.

Remember that there are also Xerox applications printing PostScript and PCL. Be on the lookout for those, too.

APA: Beyond Xerox and IBM

Round 7

By now you know that there are a lot of questions and a lot of answers. Now it's time to look at the other print datastreams that are now a regular part of business.

Do you have PostScript files?

Do you have PCL files?

Do you have PDF files?

Do you know how many variations you have?

Pay close attention to the features of these formats, and remember that they are still evolving.

Enterprise print applications generally began as mainframe-based applications on an IBM host running under MVS, though some ran under DOS/VSE or VM. These operating systems, all maintained by IBM, lent themselves to the development of applications that produced print to the IBM and Xerox printers at high speeds. Over time they added formatting capabilities, but generally as a retrofit into applications. That is why even the most recent statistics indicate that the vast majority of printing done in the corporate enterprise is line data printing generated from both in-house and purchased applications.

At the same time, most network printing developed from desktop publishing applications and network-based applications that spoke more naturally to PostScript and PCL printers. Those printers were generally considered too slow and the network applications lacked the industrial strength of their enterprise printing counterparts.

As processor speeds increased and the drive toward creating more attractive customer communication took hold, both PostScript and PCL applications began to wiggle their way into the enterprise environment. PCL printers began to pick up speed, increase their paper bin capacity, and expand their connectivity options. More PostScript printers entered the market with faster processors and the same connectivity options as the newest PCL printers. High-speed and high-capacity PostScript printers, often capable of four-color printing also emerged, often sporting roll-fed paper handling systems to handle high volume requirements. Many had IBM and Xerox logos on them.

The merging of the low-end print environments and the high-end print environments eventually drove application developers and the customers they supported to look at ways to share print responsibilities across a variety of print devices. By adding some sophisticated transform software to the application mix, it was possible to print enterprise print files to the PCL and PostScript printers on the networks and make them available on CD-ROM and the Web in Portable Document Format (PDF) and other formats.

It's important to understand how different these languages really are, however.

PostScript and PDF 101

This section covers both PostScript and PDF, but the starting point is PostScript. Adobe's PostScript is not really a printer file format. It is a page description language that is interpreted to create the raster image file that actually prints. Introduced in 1985, it was developed to allow document developers to define all of the print operators needed to completely describe a page to a printer. To provide all of the functionality needed, PostScript evolved through three language levels, each one providing additional enhancements and features.

For a complete review of all of the operations available in the PostScript language you should refer to the language manuals, which are listed in Appendix B.

The cornerstone of PostScript development is device independence. PostScript files can be routed to devices of any resolution or passed to any number of Raster Image Processing (RIP) programs. PostScript is resolution independent, which means that the PostScript code that creates a box of a specific size will print that box in the same dimensions regardless of the number of pixels in the device resolution.

So, the short story is that the PostScript language is based on the idea of interpreting the language at the device, which is usually a printer. It describes the pages and makeup, and often uses internal page macros for repeated operations. It can support everything from simple black and white printing to spot color and full color print. The good news is that it provides a lot of flexibility in the language. The bad news is that because it is a very rich language, PostScript acquired the reputation of being too slow for business printing. Today, however, with the enhanced processor speeds and increased available memory and disk on the printers, many of the concerns about PostScript have evaporated.

The PostScript language has evolved through support levels, and each level has introduced new features and variations to keep up with the evolution of the

What Can You Do With PDF?

- Post documents to the World Wide Web, a CD, intranet or extranet

- Create viewable versions of business documents

- Index, annotate, and bookmark

- Combine, extract, and manipulate document pages

output devices (printers, imagesetters, Computer-to-Plate systems), including enhanced color operators and changes in print technology. It has grown to handle most of the available font technologies and color models. Adding to the versatility, you can create print files on any platform, from mainframes to MACs, from PCs to laptops, and they are not tied to a specific operating system.

While PostScript has evolved and many devices are available to print the most current PostScript versions, it is still common to find older PostScript printers still working hard in office environments. Many are running at the older level 2 standard, and some are even older than that! To confuse matters, there are PostScript clones written by third-party vendors and printers that claim PostScript compatibility that use non-Adobe interpreters. The important point is that because there are many levels of PostScript support and additional third-party PostScript look-alikes, not all PostScript files will print on all PostScript printers.

PostScript files are generally produced by applications purchased from vendors who take on the task of keeping up with the PostScript specifications. If there is an in-house utility that generates the PostScript file, there is a risk that the PostScript may not be up to the current Adobe specifications, which limits the long-term re-usability of the output.

A PostScript Code Example

```
%!PS-Adobe-3.1
%%Title: Microsoft Word - Doc Processing Tech April2001-best
tech.doc
%%Creator: ADOBEPS4.DRV Version 4.50
%%CreationDate: 08/11/2001 10:57:55
%%For: mcgrew
%%BoundingBox: (atend)
%%Pages: (atend)
%%PageOrder: Special
%%DocumentNeededResources: (atend)
%%DocumentSuppliedResources: (atend)
%%DocumentSuppliedFeatures: (atend)
%%DocumentData: Clean7Bit
%%LanguageLevel: 2
%%TargetDevice: (Generic PostScript Printer) (2010.0) 2

%%EndComments

%%BeginDefaults
%%PageBoundingBox: 19 8 593 784
%%ViewingOrientation: 1 0 0 1
%%PageFeatures:
%%+ *InputSlot Cassette
%%+ *PageSize Letter
%%+ *PageRegion Letter
%%EndDefaults

%%BeginProlog
%%BeginResource: procset AdobePS_Win_Feature_Safe 4.2 0
userdict begin/lucas 21690 def/featurebegin{countdictstack
lucas[}bind def
/featurecleanup{stopped{cleartomark dup lucas eq{pop exit}if}loop
countdictstack exch sub dup 0 gt{{end}repeat}{pop}ifelse}bind def end
%%EndResource
%%BeginResource: procset AdobePS_FatalError 4.2 0
userdict begin/FatalErrorIf{{initgraphics findfont 1 index 0 eq{exch
pop}dup
length dict begin{1 index/FID ne{def}{pop pop}ifelse}forall/Encoding{
ISOLatin1Encoding}stopped{StandardEncoding}if def currentdict end
/ErrFont-Latin1 exch definefont}ifelse exch scalefont setfont
counttomark 3
div cvi{moveto show}repeat showpage quit}{cleartomark}ifelse}bind
def end
%%EndResource
userdict begin /PrtVMMsg {[
(This job requires more memory than is available in this printer.)
100 500
(Try one or more of the following, and then print again:) 100 485
(In the PostScript dialog box, click Optimize For Portability.) 115
470
```

A limitation of the PostScript file format was the size of the files and the amount of interpretation required by the printer. This created additional problems for Adobe when they began to get requests for a viewable form of PostScript. Designers and artists wanted to see an approximation of their work online before sending it to expensive color proofing devices. Adobe took an initial pass at creating what they called Display PostScript, but after putting significant effort into the project they came to the conclusion that the only way to create a viewable data format was to start over.

Portable Document Format - PDF

The result was a project called Carousel, the original inception of Portable Document Facility or PDF. What followed that proof of concept was the product family called Adobe Acrobat. Using either the PDF Writer, which functions as a print driver, or the PDF Distiller, which functions like a compiler to resolve the complex PostScript files into PDF, you can create a view file to verify what the ultimate print file will look like. Adobe saw this as a limited-use facility and targeted it to the graphic arts trade. But, as often happens in the market, other business segments saw that PDF had much more potential.

In the electronic document industry the PDF format looked like an answer to moving complex data formats to viewing environments in local area networks, on CD-ROMS, and later the Web. While the original PDF language specification did not provide enough flexibility to represent the complex pages normally found in enterprise print environments, as the specification matured it was possible to mimic the print image of documents originally created for printing PostScript, AFP and Xerox print environments.

Finally, Adobe changed their strategy and began enhancing PDF to meet the needs of corporate printing environments. It has become the *de facto* standard for distributing enterprise documents. The goal of today's PDF file is to preserve all of the fonts, formatting, and other elements of the document so that it both displays and prints identically. That is an important point since the original strategy was to ensure a viewing fidelity only. Today PDF shares all of the capabilities of PostScript.

The folks at Adobe say that PDF is even more reliable than PostScript, and have based their workflow solutions around it. In fact, they recommend it for every facet of document management, from prepress to archive. PDF can be viewed using a the free Acrobat Reader, or you can build a more substantial viewing environment using Adobe's Acrobat product set that includes a applications to catalog a library of PDF documents and to scan and save paper documents. The current versions of the most popular Web Browsers support PDF viewing, too.

If you have applications generating print formats it may not be convenient to push files through PC-based print drivers. Coming to the rescue are any number of vendors providing transform and migration tools to move existing print file formats to PDF, often with the ability to add navigation and search capability to the files as part of the transform. Many of these vendors are listed in Appendix C.

PCL 101

In the corporate world, there are thousands, if not hundreds of thousands, of printers that accept the Hewlett Packard Print Control Language print format, commonly known as PCL. Some are from HP and many more are from other manufacturers who support the PCL datastream. Just as in the PostScript environment, it will be important to understand exactly what type of PCL printers and print applications you are working with.

PCL has evolved over the years through at least six distinct support levels, with many variations along the way. HP says that PCL levels 1 through 5 are compatible, but PCL Level 6 is a radically different version that uses different commands to talk with the printer. See the HP site and their reference manuals for more details.

Most of the PCL print language is based on the use of an escape character, often ASCII 27, followed by specific coding sequences in the print data to control the formatting of the print. This coding not only varies a bit among the various levels of PCL, but can also be tied to specific printer models. And, as HP has progressed through the levels, it has become more complex.

In addition to the simple and complex escape sequences, PCL supports the use of macros to create small object blocks that can be re-executed in a print file. If your organization has written macros that are used in your print files, be ready for challenges if you attempt to move the print files to other environments. The success of the migration will depend on how accurately the transform or migration program can read and interpret the macros, and reproduce the visual results.

Another facet of the HP PCL environment is that many of the printers allowed the use of fonts that were resident on cartridges that resided physically in the printer. Many companies took advantage of the cartridges to have logos, signatures and other corporate graphics encoded as fonts or downloadable forms and made available on only those printers designated by an administrator. It also allowed companies to adopt the use of non-standard fonts in their documents. The challenge is that the information about what is actually on the cartridge does not usually reside anywhere in the print file. A font or logo may only be referred to as a file name. It is another of those issues that you want to know about before you attempt to move files to a new print environment.

The good news is that most companies have abandoned the cartridges and altered the print applications to ensure that all of the information needed to print the file resides on a server or within the print file. If you know that there are printers in your environment that have used cartridges, spend some extra time as you review the print environment and print the files to some alternative printer to ensure that there are no potential problems with cartridge-based information.

In addition to the escape sequences in the PCL print file, there is also the possibility that there will be graphics in the file. Some graphics are included files, but others are created using HP's Graphic language, HP-GL/2. Since not all printers support the language, and many PCL transform programs do not support the graphic commands, it will be important to know if you have applications and documents that use HP GL/2.

You should also determine if your files use the HP Printer Job Language (PJL) to control copy counts, simplex and duplex functions, as well as input and output bin selection. Again, since not all printers support the commands, and not all printers use the same command strings, there is room for variation within your enterprise. As with the graphic language, PJL is generally not supported in its entirety by the transform and migration programs that accept PCL as input.

In the PCL environment we used to be able to say that the files were generated from a PC or network environment, but during the 1990s there was an surge in the number of applications running on IBM mainframes, UNIX processors, and AS/400 systems supporting PCL output to high-speed PCL printers and to integrated networks of PCL printers. Because PCL can be generated from any environment it is important to learn about the sources of your PCL and any existing programs or routines that might be in place to alter the PCL for your business environment.

With the groundwork laid we are ready to move on to the largest problem we face when working with print data in the digital world. Fonts.

We are not finished considering the data yet, but before we can address the remaining challenges it is necessary to understand how we make the data look the way we want.

Fonts

Round 8

Since what you see on the page is the direct result of the fonts used to print the data, you need to pay close attention to the way the fonts are constructed and how they are specified in the print files. Here is a longer look at all of the font file variations.

What types of fonts do you have?

Who makes decisions about what fonts can be used?

How do you make good font decisions?

Remember that in most environments there are many font file formats in use.

What is the real output of all of your applications?

For most business applications the output is some type of document that formats the information to be delivered to the recipient so that they can make use of it. Invoices, user manuals, bank statements, and insurance policies all share this characteristic. They are created to provide information to someone, usually so that they can take some action, such as paying the bill, using a product, or verifying their assets.

In the computer, all of the data is stored in massive databases and disk files. The formats are appropriate for the computer and the applications, but not for usability. It takes the mapping of the information in the computer or produced by the applications to a print or view format to make it all usable. Fonts are the mechanism that do that. How they are used in a document creates an impression about the document, which is both good and bad. After all, for most business documents the *fonts* are **not** the message.

The Backgrounder

Let's start with the word FONT.

It may be the most hated and most feared term in the information delivery industry. You might have thought it was *network* or *backbone* or *router*, but those are technical issues that generally have tangible answers. FONT, on the other hand, presents the hardest of problems because everyone sees things just a little bit differently. Corporations have favorite fonts, logo fonts, and corporate image fonts. Art Directors have strong opinions, and print programmers have opinions of their own.

At the baseline is the concept of applying a unique image pattern to each letter, number and symbol in an alphanumeric symbol set. This gets a bit tricky when you are talking about fonts that incorporate graphic elements or portions of a corporate logo, but in the end, the font is the unique combination of characters, and in our world of printing and viewing, they are manifested in a file, or set of coordinated files. If you've been with us from the start of the book, this is old news.

A font is also the specific instance of a typeface. For instance, Arial is a typeface, but Arial 11-point bold is a font. There are thousands of fonts, some specifically designed for flowing text, others designed for headlines or advertising. The important point is that not all fonts are made for all purposes. Let's look at them in a bit more depth.

Text vs. Display Fonts

This is a nice text font...

CHIS IS HARDER CO READ

Fonts come in proportional and fixed variations.
Proportional fonts let the widths of the characters vary,
while fixed pitch fonts use a uniform character width.

Monospaced Characters

```
1234567890    ABCDEFGHIJKLMNOPQRSTUVWXYZ

0987654321    abcdefghijklmnopqrstuvwxyz
```

For many business applications the fixed-pitch font solved the problem of getting numbers to line up in columns. You see them used in almost every industry, in applications like insurance declaration pages and policies as well as pharmaceutical data sheets, manufacturing specifications, and all types of accounting applications. For many years there were not good fixed-pitch equivalents in the desktop printing or typesetting environments, but most vendors now supply fixed-pitch or pseudo-fixed pitch fonts to meet user requests. Pseudo-fixed pitch fonts have uniform width characters but may not use a fixed width for inter-word spaces.

Fixed-pitch fonts emulate the action of the oldest typewriters, where every character had exactly the same height and width, and the inter-character spacing was always identical. Courier is the most common fixed-pitch font when you leave the IBM and Xerox print worlds, though there are fonts like Lucida Console and MS Terminal that often provide good matches. When any of them are used to replace one of the IBM or Xerox fixed-pitch fonts, there are a variety of situations where the replacement font characteristics are out of proportion with the original fonts. When the replacement font is wider, characters may exceed the display boundaries or print boundaries of the new environment. As always, as your wrestle the data make your decisions and then test to be sure that your final output meets your requirements.

A Font by Any Other Name...

A font is a set of characters or symbols sharing a *typeface*. Typefaces are often characterized as *serif* or *sans serif*. *Serif* fonts share a characteristic tail on each character, while *sans serif* typefaces are cleaner, sharper iterations of the characters with adornment. While these general characterizations hold for most fonts, there are also *pseudo* serif and sans serif fonts that exhibit most of the characteristics, but may violate some the basic tenets.

At the risk of becoming a text on font design, we will leave that idea there and go on to some of the other terms you will encounter in a font discussion. Next are the terms *roman*, *italic* and *oblique*. These refer to the stress of the typeface. Roman fonts are basically square to the baseline, while italic and oblique fonts are stressed to the left or right.

All fonts have weight characteristics that identify the lightness or darkness of the type representation. Most fonts that we work with are normal or bold, but there are fonts from extra light to ultra bold in many font catalogs.

Many fonts represent an instance of the typeface at a specific physical size, represented in *points*. A printer's point is approximately 1/72nd of an inch. The point size of a font can be deceiving, however, because of how fonts are measured. To determine a font's point size, measure from the top of the tallest character, called an *ascender*, to the bottom of the lowest hanging character, called a *decender*. Sounds simple enough, but it's possible for two 11-point fonts to look quite different.

Fonts may be contained in font files that contain a bitmap image of each character with the appropriate amount of space left above, below, and beside the character to make it display or print as needed. Other bitmap font files contain no additional space around the characters and anticipate that the software that uses the font will fill in that detail. Because bitmap fonts contain the actual images of each character you must have a separate font file for each size type font you require.

Still other fonts are stored as a program of vectors that cause the image of the characters to be drawn as needed. Because these are scalable you need fewer files to convey the needed type fonts to the paper or screen. Adobe introduced a family of these types of fonts as MultiMaster fonts, which allows PostScript and PDF to condense the amount of information they need within the text file to produce the font on the screen or on the printer as expected. There are also other formats that use the idea of scaling the font within a range of point sizes.

For most of the last 20 years and more of high-speed corporate printing we have relied on raster fonts, but slowly vector, scalable fonts are coming into use in enterprise documents. This is good news because it makes it easier to match older raster fonts when you can specify an 11.5-point font instead of just an 11-point or 12-point font. The point size is not the only issue, however.

How we perceive the point size is based on the x-height of the font. The x-height is exactly what it sounds like; it is the height of the lowercase x in the font. Depending on the type designer the x-height may be only 1/3 of the height of a t or l, or it may be ¾ of the height. Type designers sometimes make the ascenders excessively high or chop off the decenders, which also changes the overall appearance of the font. So, as you look at fonts, pay attention to more than just the size as stated in the font specifications. Look at how the font really prints.

Comparing X Heights

gxt gxt
GXT GXT

Print resolution plays a part in how fonts print since the number of pixels or dots-per-square-inch that are available to resolve the font determines its appearance. On a computer screen that is measured in pixels, with an average of 72 or 96 pixels-squared-per-square-inch. Compare that to the 240 dpi on older AFP printers, 300 dpi on older Xerox high-speed printers, and 600 dpi on newer printers in AFP, Xerox and PostScript/PDF product lines. Now imagine what happens when fonts designed for a 300 or 600 dpi resolution are moved to 240 dpi devices or to a screen.

This will be one of the challenges as print files move to new platforms. The other is to remember the legal issues. Typefaces and fonts are copyrighted and, often, trademarked. To use them requires a license, which sometimes restricts what you can do with a font. For example, if you look at the license agreements on many of the *free* fonts or fonts contained on an inexpensive font CD, you'll discover that the fonts cannot be used for commercial purposes. Examine the license agreements on fonts from the major font vendors and you often find that the use of the fonts is limited to a specific type of printer or a specific resolution. Some font vendors do not release their font for use on devices that they believe change the way the font appears. If you are using custom-built font sets, this could be a challenge you will face in opening up your print to alternative delivery devices.

At the lowest level, there are character sets, which determine what characters are available to print. Character sets are often linked to an independent codepage, which is the master mapping table of the hex value that exists in the print data file to the character's raster pattern which actually prints. In the IBM world, the character sets and codepages are independent files that are mapped together, while in the Xerox world the font files contain the raster images of the characters and their mapping as a single unit. You'll see more about this in a moment.

Remember that not all characters are available in all fonts. A Times Roman font purchased from one vendor may have all of the characters needed to produce all of the Latin-based romance languages, but if purchased from another vendor they may not. This will be another item to add to the testing checklist.

The relationship between the characters is determined by the font metrics. This gets back to the x-height concept. The metrics codify how much space is left between the characters, how big the characters are at a specific point size, and how they will behave when programs that try to manipulate the inter-character and inter-line spacing are used.

Font Challenges

Monetary symbols: $, ¥, £, ¢,
Punctuation: ¿, ˜, !
NLS character sets: À, Á, Â, Ã, Ä, Å, Æ, Ð, Ø, ñ, Ç, ß
Legal designations: §, ®, ©
Custom fonts: ◆ ✳ ❄ ❱ ▲ ✚ ✖ ❀ ✕ ✓ ❖ ❚ ✘ ∞

Font Hurdles

Here is where we find the hurdles on the road to moving legacy data and having it appear in the new media in the same manner as it appeared in the original medium. The variety of fonts developed for printing on high-speed laser printers (or even older impact printers) was restricted due to memory considerations on the printer CPUs and disk space available on the printers or their support CPUs. Each manufacturer developed a set of fonts. If you print on IBM printers you used their fonts, and if you print on Xerox printers you use their fonts. Because the IBM fonts were originally developed for 240 dpi printers and the Xerox fonts for 300 dpi printers, you don't find too many similar fonts across the environments.

By the mid-to-late 1980s there were many more shops trying to develop multi-vendor print solutions, which gave birth to a number of companies and tools for making fonts available on alternative devices. The truth is that many of the 240 dpi fonts did not translate well to 300 dpi, nor did the 300 dpi fonts translate well to the 240 dpi environment. To this day in multi-vendor print environments you often see some differences in the character shapes, inter-character spacing, and even the line spacing.

Delivery to the screen makes life even harder because you have a nominal 72 dpi to work with and a vast array of display devices, video drivers and screen sizes. Is the delivery intended for a 640x480 low-end VGA screen or a 1024x768 high-end SVGA screen, or something in the middle? Depending on the fonts used in your corporate documents and the nature of your corporate logos you may find that representation at such a low resolution is somewhat disappointing.

So, what can you do?

Identify all of the fonts you use in your corporate environment. This goes back to those lists you made at the start of your mission. Identify how many fall into the category of *printer-specific* fonts supplied by the vendor. Then identify the fonts that appear to have Windows equivalents. Those are fonts like Helvetica, Times Roman, and Courier. If you have a font/type expert on board, they can help you through the strange mappings, like using Helvetica for Helios, or Optima for Oracle. Sometimes very similar fonts have a number of names depending on the type foundry they were acquired from. Times Roman, Times, TMS Roman, and Times New Roman are not identical, but are similar enough that you can start by treating them as if they are identical.

Now to the hard part. Look carefully and try to determine how important a specific font is to your documents. If you transform your Xerox or AFP print file to HTML or PDF, but the fonts look odd, try to decide if you can change to a more display-friendly font?

What are your options? They are getting better every day. Today you could distribute an embedded font in a PDF file to guarantee that the font you want used actually displays on the viewer's screen. Or, you could use one of a number of proprietary technologies to embed fonts into HTML files. Microsoft, Bitstream and others have a number of interesting ways to ensure that you have the font image you want. Of course, if the font you want just doesn't look good on the screen, you still have that tough decision. As a rule the pseudo-sans serif fonts like Optima and Oracle do not look as good when translated to the web. You'll find that corporate logos with fine detail may not look as good as you'd like either. We will return to this point at the end of the chapter.

Vendor Specific Font Issues

The primary print file formats you encounter in big corporate environments are plain text formats (sometimes with a few twists), IBM's AFP, and the Xerox DJDE and Metacode. AFP and the Xerox formats use specific font formats, and line data or plain text may have fonts attached through the use of an external print control file. You cannot use the nice Book Antiqua or Comic Sans copied from your PC and use it in a corporate report destined for print on the company AFP or Xerox printer. The printer and its software will not understand the information in the file.

IBM Fonts

IBM fonts have many variations, so you will need to track down which ones you have and use to get ready for any migration. The oldest style of IBM font is the type that supported their oldest line print devices (many of which are still in use). You'll find these fonts used in *line data* files that look remarkably like what you might have produced in a typewriter. Fonts in a line data format are designated by their position in a font list that is carried with the job. The important part is that the print stream calls for fonts by number, but whether it is font number three or font number four isn't nearly as important to us as what fonts are on that font list, and what format the font files are in. By format we mean the character set, the resolution, and information about how the inter-character and inter-word spacing is handled. In these older style fonts you will often see names like Elite and Prestige, reminiscent of the old typewriter balls from the early electric typewriters and word processing systems. Note the name of any font you see identified because you may need to try to match it to a web font down the road.

AFP Fonts...

Font 3800/38PP & GraphMod
PSF Compatibility Fonts: GT10, Prestige, etc.
   Font 3820 and the Sonoran Family: Coded Fonts
   separate raster pattern from character set
        Sonoran Family, Pi & Specials, Data1, APL2,
        Math & Science (5771s)
Core Interchange Families: Based on ATM outline fonts
AFP Fonts Version 2 (5448 & 5648)
        -- bitmap and outline: Times New Roman, Helvetica,
        Courier + 4 fixed pitch fonts
AFP fonts have three parts that exist in separate files.
  • C0 members contain the bitmaps of the fonts
  • T1 members are codepages - hex value locations
     for characters
  • X0 members are "coded fonts" which contain the
     cross referenced names of a C0 and a T1 member.
Documents refer to fonts by name using either the C0
   and the T1 name or only using the X0 name.

Fonts	Issues	Web Matches
IBM3800	Most are designed for system printing and don't look very good when ported to the web.	None
GraphMod	Systems programmers created these fonts, usually as logos and signatures for use in check and policy applications. It is very difficult to convert these to web fonts. The best bet is to alter the program to use a graphic format instead.	None
IBM3820	This is the next generation at 240 dpi, mostly based on Adobe original masters, hand-tuned to look good on the IBM 240 dpi printers. If the Pi and Specials font is used to access data processing characters you will have some challenges.	Helvetica Times New Roman
PSF Compatibility Fonts	These were created by IBM to make migration from their line printers to their high-speed laser printers easier. These fonts have names like GT10, GT12, Prestige, and OCR-A, which match most of those fonts you saw in older line printer applications. Check any applications relying on rows and columns of numbers to line up very carefully.	None
Newest Fonts	The new generations of IBM fonts are built with the assumption that they are needed for printing and viewing applications. Check your list of fonts carefully and see how many appear to be PC-based fonts. Do not, however, assume that all of the characters will be included in the character set. Remember to check every page that you convert to ensure that currency symbols and other special characters appear in the output.	None
Unmentionables	For the sake of covering all of the bases, people put all sorts of things into font files. Signatures, flow charts, pie charts, corporate logos, and just about anything else. Remember that any of these special fonts will need some web equivalent; it may not be easy to get there!	None

The older printers used fonts that resided in a single file that contained all of the information the printer needed, but as the printers became more sophisticated, the font handling method changed. As newer printers were introduced IBM defined a set of file formats that allowed the character sets to be carried in one file, the codepage that mapped hex values to raster patterns in another file, and then a third format (called a Coded Font) that mapped together a character set and code page into a font resource to be used by the printer.

That did set up a point of risk since it is possible for the Coded Font to call for a character set or code page that it does not have access to, causing an error in the print job.

In the AFP environment, the character sets are easily found by their eight character name beginning in C0. The IBM documentation explains how you can derive the font information from the name of the font. The codepages are also easy to identify by the T1 prefix. Coded Fonts are prefixed with X0.

Codepages and character sets work together to provide the alphabetics, numerics, and symbols. There are language-specific character sets and language-specific codepages, but there are also country-specific codepages. For example, there are separate codepages for US English and UK English. If a print job references a codepage that has an invalid or missing code point you normally see errors for the print job.

Beware, though. However, in our many years of working with print data we have seen production print jobs that produced errors everyday and were never repaired. Just be aware that because something is in production does not mean that it is a perfect job!

The first of the IBM fonts to use the character set-codepage-coded font combination arrived with the dawn of AFP printing in the middle 1980s. IBM distributed a font group called the *PSF Compatibility Fonts*, which were designed to allow the users of their newest printers to continue printing the jobs they had already created, with little or no change to the code that was in use. You'll know these fonts by looking for names like GT-10, GT-12, Prestige, or OCR-A.

Fonts from this era were built with the specific requirements of older data in mind, so they do pose some challenges as you try to migrate to the web.

The next generation, the IBM Sonoran family of Typographic fonts were intended to provide a complete font family that the document designer could use reliably to get great looking documents from their high-speed printer. IBM faced a small challenge in that their printers were running at 240 dpi while most of their competitors were running at 300 dpi or more. That meant that IBM had to shave pixels out of their font characters yet still appear to achieve perfect, art-director approvable print.

A Quick Word About the IBM Sonoran Family

If you work with documents that still use the IBM Sonoran font set, you may have a few challenges. We mentioned in earlier sections that the Sonoran family was built specifically for the IBM 240 dpi printers, beginning with the IBM 3820 in the 1980s. The Sonoran fonts have each character hand-kerned for 240 dpi printing, which was the standard for IBM AFP printers when the fonts were created. The transform from 240 dpi to 300 or 600 dpi is not that difficult, but matching the kerning that was done to ensure that all of the characters looked their best at 240 is almost impossible to match. The net result is that selecting alternative fonts often uncovers several problems.

Mapping Sonoran Sans Serif to Helvetica, the logical choice, poses a challenge because the Sonoran Sans Serif font is narrower. Because the characters are wider in the Helvetica font, they slide together in the larger point sizes, and take up more horizontal space for the same number of characters. In applications where the text is dense, such as insurance policies, MSDS forms, and tables in user manuals, the original tight fit turns into "no fit" in the new environment. The problem intensifies when the original application kerned the text to squeeze it even tighter.

The challenges are a bit different with Sonoran Serif,

which we normally map to New Times Roman. When we replace a Sonoran Serif 10-point with a 10-point Times font, sometimes the text is too narrow to the eye. If we go to an 11-point font the text actually looked much better, and generally fits.

You might encounter Sonoran Petite and Sonoran Display, which were special purpose fonts. The Sonoran Petite is a tiny font, and it would not translate well to any viewing environment. Sonoran Display was designed to handle requirements for large fonts, such as titles and headings.

It helps to know that IBM began with the Monotype Helvetica font when creating the Sans Serif font and the New Times Roman when creating the Serif font. We did not get to use those specific fonts only because Monotype and IBM couldn't come to an arrangement.

IBM followed the Sonorans with the Core Interchange Fonts, which included a family of familiar fonts such as Helvetica and Times. IBM encouraged customers to migrate their applications to use the new fonts during the late 1980s. If you took their advice, you are well positioned to make the leap to new output environments. If you didn't, you have a much tougher path.

The latest generation of IBM fonts have moved on to Adobe outline technology, so you will generally find that documents created using fonts with the familiar names like Arial, New Century School Book, and Times are based on the same masters as those fonts you are familiar with on your desktop. That makes our job a lot easier. Let's stop in the IBM realm with the requirement to make a list of every font you think might be used in a print file. Talk to your System administrators and find out what fonts are in the test and production font libraries, which will be the best place to start. If the fonts are in those libraries, they can end up in one of your documents.

Xerox Fonts

Now let's look at the Xerox environment. Here things look quite a bit different because the folks at Xerox settled on a standard font tape early in their support of laser printing. If you were a North American client you became the proud owner of the A03 tape, and in Europe you received the R03 tape. These tapes contained font files in standard Xerox font file format for fonts that Xerox thought that you would

Fonts	Issues	Web Matches
.FNT	Xerox fonts usually live in the world at 300 dpi. The printer came with software to permit users to add characters to fonts, combine fonts, and delete standard fonts from the machines, all of which you can find in any given shop. This means that for every Xerox printer, high-speed or low-speed, you will need a list of fonts that are stored on the machine. For many Xerox fonts, especially those purchased from Xerox or one of their third party vendors as a complete font family, locating web matches is very easy. Most turn out to be standard Adobe fonts. For anything that was done as a custom font, though, you will want to be very careful checking the test output of the jobs using the fonts.	None
.LGO	Xerox has a font format that they call .LGO to handle logos and signatures as fonts on their machines. That means that where you find LGO files you will be looking for some way to find a web equivalent.	None

Setting Fonts in a DJDE

```
$$XEROX
JDL=MMJDL,FONTS=(UN110E,PO6BOB,PR211E),DUPLEX=NO,;

$$XEROX JDE=ONLINE,FORMAT=FRM9,END;
```

use to build your forms and documents. They also tried to
emulate fonts that they expected you might have used in
your line printer data, and tried to provide a sampling of
typographic fonts.

Xerox Fonts...

A03/R03 fonts: Raster pattern and character set in a
single file

Not a complete font family in the set

Encrypted fonts

.FNT families: Helvetica, Century Schoolbook...

.LGO files

Where the IBM fonts live in a library on that big mainframe
or network server that hums along in MIS, the Xerox folks
took a different approach and the fonts became part of
the system files on each individual printer. The logic was
that while IBM printers were true system printers, always
attached to the mainframe computer, the Xerox printers
could be set up to run in *offline* mode in printer farms. As
long as you kept all of the fonts you owned, including those
you created or purchased, on every machine, you could
print any job at any time on any machine. This was a huge
selling point, but it is also the source of a few challenges if
you have Xerox printers.

Let's start with the fact that Xerox was making several types
of printers at the time, and they did not share file formats
or font formats. These big, high-speed machines sometimes
came with a free *XES* (Xerox Escape Sequence) machine.
We talked about the XES format in the chapter on Xerox
printing, and what you should have taken away from that
discussion is that XES is a totally different format. While
Xerox would should you how to use the XES printers for
office printing and sometimes job proofing, the XES printers
used a completely different set of fonts. For our purposes,
we are going to concentrate on the non-XES font issues.

Adobe Base 14

Courier (Regular, Bold, Italic, and Bold Italic)

Arial MT (Regular, Bold, Oblique, and Bold Oblique)*

Times New Roman PS MT (Roman, Bold, Italic, and Bold
   Italic)*

Symbol

ZapfDingbats

   * Used to include Helvetica instead of Arial and Times
   instead of Times New Roman as part of Base 14 set prior
   to Acrobat 4.0.

Getting back to the A03/R03 font set, you will have to do
some investigation of your applications. On that A03/R03
tape Xerox included subsets of a number of font families.
You had some font files that were upper case only. Other
fonts were supplied in only one or two point sizes, often
without italic or bold versions. All of you who have
applications built with these fonts know that it was often
a challenge to find a combination of fonts that would
meet your print formatting needs. In some cases, the print
programmers resorted to adding characters to standard font
files or writing the applications to switch fonts in the middle
of words to meet the application requirements.

To meet increasing demand for more complete font
families, Xerox font packages based on the Adobe Outlines.
They made Univers, Helvetica, Century Schoolbook and
other popular fonts available, but never went back and filled
in the font families on the A03 or R03 font tapes. Another
point is that the Univers on the original Xerox font tapes
does not match the Univers sold later in the font packages.
So, take care with fonts from this era. Remember that even
these fonts based on outlines are still raster fonts. They do
not scale.

Target Font Technologies

Legacy data will most commonly use raster fonts, but the output environment may use raster or vector technology to image the information. The interesting thing about output to the Web and other next generation devices is that you sometimes lose control of the fonts entirely.

If you are converting documents to PDF, you can specify fonts to be included in the PDF file or you can reference fonts that you assume will be available in the display environment. Many PDF files are created to assume that the core set of Adobe fonts will be available, and embed any fonts that are not part of the base 14 set. If you do not specify the fonts in the PDF file, then Acrobat and your web browser start making decisions for you.

The same thing happens with HTML and XML pages that do not specify fonts, or that specify fonts that you do not have on your PC. You see the defaults and the document may not look the way you intended.

To help you engage in a dialog with your applications designers and document designers, it helps to know that most output environments today support TrueType and Adobe font formats, and many also support OpenType. Many screen display environments are now supporting OpenType, an extension of TrueType that incorporates PostScript support, too.

Here are the basic formats you want to become familiar with:

- Type 1 scalable outline fonts with hints, compatible with Adobe Type Manager (ATM); include CFF (Compact Font Format)
- Type 3 raster fonts; file contains the text "FontType 3def"
- Extended Font Set in PostScript Level 3 extends the base font set to 136 fonts and adds Central and Eastern European characters
- OpenType (TrueType Open V 2.0) is an extension of the TrueType font format, adding support for

PostScript font data. OpenType was developed jointly by Microsoft and Adobe to provide users with a simple way to install and use fonts, whether the fonts contain TrueType outlines or CFF (PostScript) outlines.

Now let's make one last pass through the font world with an eye on finding your potential problem areas.

What You Have

Regardless of the vendor, the older the font, the more likely you will encounter problems moving documents that use them to any new output environment. If you are starting with fonts originally designed for typewriters, impact printers, and the earliest laser printers, the chances of finding exact matches for your fonts are slim, but improving.

A number of companies have stepped in to create font sets to mimic the Xerox A03 and R03 fonts set, the IBM compatibility fonts, and even the original typewriter fonts such as Prestige, Elite and Gothic, but your success at using them relies on how perfect a match you require.

Which brings us to another point. Many organizations have policies in place that do not permit fonts to be altered or special fonts to be purchased, usually out of concern for portability. Even if you work in one of those organizations, it is common to find custom fonts in production because signatures and logos are often converted to font files to improve print speed and enhance security.

If you are using transform software to migrate your output to a new platform, that software may take care of you by rasterizing the font into a the appropriate raster pattern in the new output environment. If the resulting output meets your quality standards, you've met the challenge. If it doesn't, or you use a solution that does not offer the option, your next solution involves creating a version of the font in the new environment.

You can improve your chances of a smooth migration if you have access to the font vendor that provided any custom fonts. They can often provide a Windows-compatible font in TrueType or ATM format, since most began with PC-based fonts and transformed them into formats compatible with the target printer.

If you decide to try one of the windows-based font sets that emulate production or custom Xerox and IBM font sets, take some extra time to test and review. Verify that every character that you use is represented in the new font file, and that it prints as expected in your new output environment. This is critical in organizations that took advantage of the font editing software available to add and modify characters in the fonts.

Can't find the original vendor? Depending on how *custom* the font is, you might be able to find another vendor who can make the font for you. For example, a well-known rental company had commissioned a font with all of the interstate road signs a number of years ago and when they wanted to move to a new delivery environment (PDF) they found that they could buy a set that would work for them.

Another resource is the Xplor Font Bank (www.xplor.com), where you can find a wide range of possible font matches. Be careful if you go this route and test diligently since the code points for each character (the hex value at which the character is located within the font file) may not be identical.

Your next best solution is to have your existing font files converted to the appropriate format, or do it yourself. Companies like Terrapin Software (www.terrapin.co.uk) have vast expertise working with both IBM AFP fonts and Xerox fonts, as do ASE Technologies (www.ase-tech.com).

If you want to step up to converting fonts yourself, try the folks at Lytrod Software (www.lytrod.com) and their BitCopy software. BitCopy can create fonts for AFP, Xerox, PCL, PostScript/PDF (Type 1), TrueType, and FastFont formats. They also have a font editor that lets you change global parameters for a font or edit a specific character. This same product lets you work with Xerox LGO (Logo) files, AFP Page Segment files, GIFs, TIFFs and PCX files and transform them into the format you require.

And don't forget products like Fontographer or the IBM Type Transformer, and others like them that provide paths for creating fonts. If you go this route, be sure you understand the legal implications of moving fonts to new platforms.

The thrust here is that you can get a working version of an existing font. At the risk of making an obvious statement, the problem in moving legacy data to the web while relying on these font solutions is that the end user has to have those same fonts available on their PC or they will see the default font established for their machine and not the font you intended for your information presentation. It can be a perfect solution for an intranet, but a harder solution to ensure fidelity for when you move out on to the World Wide Web and beyond.

What do you do if you have a font you need and you can't trust the environment of the target reader of the web page? One option depends on the software you use for your migration to the web. If you purchase a solution, you can often invoke a parameter that will transform any font to bitmap images within the output file. This is primarily for PostScript and PDF output solutions, and it can be the perfect answer for scientific and industry-specific fonts or corporate logo fonts. It will make the resulting PDF file a bit larger, but you will have fidelity.

Solutions from Solimar (www.solimarsystems.com), Xenos (www.xenos.com), Emtex (www.emtex.com), CSP (www.csp.de), Elixir Technologies (www.elixir.com), Rochester Software Associates (www.rocsoft.com), and ePage (formerly SysPrint, Inc. - www.sysprint.com), and others are also candidates for getting through the font problems in a legacy-to-the-web conversion. (See Appendix C for a more complete list of vendors.)

Along with these solutions, if you want to go it alone you can look at font embedding technology from companies like Bitstream or a technology from Microsoft called WEFT (Web Embedding Font Technology), that may solve your problems. With WEFT, a link is established to font objects in your web page that are hosted at your site or at your ISP. It's not a trivial process to build, but it will give you fidelity. Check out the Microsoft site at www.microsoft.com/typography for more information on how it works and for a copy of the WEFT specifications.

We'll say it again. FONT. The four letter expletive of the document industry. No magic bullets. No easy answers. This one is going to be a judgment call.

Suggestions

The more you learn about the fonts in use in your print applications, the more you may be appalled. Remember, though that print jobs grow organically and often under impossible deadlines. Your predecessors did what they had to do to get the job done. That does not mean that you cannot develop a plan to modernize your font infrastructure, however. Here are some suggestions:

- If you have legacy applications using older style fonts, use the next maintenance cycle to update the fonts and test.

- Eliminating custom fonts, fonts that use edited codepages, and fonts that use unusual spacing also contributes to the longevity of documents.

- If you are using custom fonts, look at them carefully to see if there is a standard font that will do the job just as well.

- If you have applications that use shading done with fonts or place graphics as fonts, use the next maintenance cycle to correct the situation. And then, test!

- If you use fonts like the Monotype Sorts, WingDings or a symbol font, check that your document looks the same on all anticipated platforms.

- If you are using barcode and edgemark fonts, test the output if you change printers or reprint from a viewing environment or the Web.

- Replacing older fonts with fonts based on ATM or TrueType fonts makes the document more versatile.

Graphics

Round 9

In this chapter, we are looking at the graphics, which may be included inline in the print stream or called by a reference. They might be stored in a mainframe library or on a printer disk. By the end of this chapter you should be able to converse with the people who manage the graphic resources and understand their answers.

What types of graphics do you use and who is responsible for them?

What graphics are the most critical?

When you do your graphics inventory don't forget to poll all of the departments to determine if there are legal or political issues associated with the graphic files.

In the last chapter we took a hard look at fonts, and as good a start as that makes, we still have to take a good look at another resource: graphics.

The term *graphics* means a lot of different things to different constituents. For the purposes of legacy data, you will find that there are vendor-specific graphic file formats and there are graphics encoded into font formats. We did all of these things to ourselves in the quest for faster-printing files, and now we have to dig our way back out.

Let us start with the obvious; the vendor-specific graphic file formats you are likely to encounter.

In a Xerox environment, there are several variations in the DJDE/Metacode environments, and there are those XES/UDK machines still in use in many places. The most common Xerox printers, though, are the high-speed printers, usually printing on cut-sheet paper, that were born with the Xerox 8700 using line data mixed with Dynamic Job Descriptor Entries (DJDEs) or Xerox Metacode to achieve print. In this environment, your graphics may be embedded in a font, encoded in a file format called a LOGO (extension .LGO), or created as an Image file (extension .IMG). Since the very first incarnation of the 8700s had limited disk space and limited memory, Xerox tried to find ways to encode graphics into the files using the least amount of the available processing resource. This was the birth of the use of the font file format to place a graphic on the printed page.

The limitation on using a font file to place a graphic image is that you must have your composition program, whatever it might be, make the call to the font file and place the specific characters containing the pieces of the graphic into the output print. Not impossible, but not trivial. To make it a bit easier Xerox provided the .LGO format, which is a Xerox font file in which the graphic characters are pre-loaded. That means you simply call the .LGO file and the graphic appears in the output. Sounds great and works great. It is, however, difficult to migrate. The problem is that the web and its sister formats really don't understand the .LGO file format, let alone the Xerox font file format, so we have to make some decisions about the best way to get that graphic into the new output file.

Xerox also supports a raster file format called an .IMG file (not to be confused with .IMG files from some PC graphic programs). As the Xerox machines became faster and included higher storage and memory capacity, the use of the raster file format became more popular. More and

Graphics	Issues	Web
MO:DCA	Many people we've encountered talk about having **MO:DCA** graphics in their files. What they really mean is that they have one of the two formats listed below.	
IOCA	IOCA has gone through changes over the years, so watch for file creation dates and what products were used. Inside IOCA you can have several different image formats, like IM1, Function set 10, function set 11, and function set 42. Not all are supported by all printers or transforms.	Same as PSEG
GOCA	For a vector graphic format that gave you small files, it never became as popular across the board in AFP environments. However, you do have to watch for it and you do need to understand what created it.	None

more graphic programs were able to produce the format, and graphics dotted more and more of the output print files. Again, though, this raster file format has a bunch of variations and is still distinctively a Xerox file format. You don't just ask your web browser to take a look at it and render it; most cannot.

And remember, all of this involves raster data (bitmaps) for the graphics. There is not a Xerox vector file format, so these files grow as the size of the graphic image grows. Xerox raster files and font/logo files are stored at 300 dpi in most cases, though some machines support 600 dpi. The larger the graphic, the higher the resolution, the larger the file, the slower the print. Truisms of the Xerox graphic world.

Moving on to the Advanced Function Printing Environment, we also find graphics encoded into one of the font formats, or contained in something called a Page Segment (PSEG or .PSG) file. In the beginning this was a wrapper for a raster file format, but over time as the Advanced Function Printing Architecture grew, it became a wrapper for additional raster formats and vector formats as well. You may find PSEGS encoded at resolution of 240 dpi, 300 dpi, and even 1200 dpi resolutions. Yes, that means you have to be on the lookout for everything.

Graphics	Issues	Web
Xerox .FNT	There are normally 300 dpi files containing text characters, but in some cases customers coded graphics into the character values to create corporate logos that would print faster than a raster graphic	Make a font that matched, -- you have to ensure it is available to every machine's browser or encode the font into the HTML/PDF file.
Xerox .LGO	The Logo files are really font files with a bit more information in them. They identify the order of the characters needed to create the graphic correctly.	Same as above.
Xerox .IMG	This is a raster file format that is normally at 300 dpi but at 600 dpi in some cases. IMGs were traditionally black and white, but color has been creeping in rapidly over the past five years, so watch out for all possibilities.	
IBM PSEG3820	While most PSEG files contain 240 dpi black and white graphics, there have been many variations over the years. Watch for creation dates and the products used to create the page segments. The more you know about what created them the easier it will be to make web equivalents. As above, you will have to get the file into a web compatible format.	Same as above.

Since IBM not only makes printers, but also lots of software, there were always products in the mainframe shops capable of producing some type of graphic file format, and most could be edited into something that the AFP printers will print. AFP PSEG files can not only wrap raw raster data for printing, but also a number of additional AFP architectural components, such as IOCA (Image Object Content Architecture) files, which are a raster format, and GOCA (Graphic Object Content Architecture) files, which are vector format.

The oldest files will probably be pure black and white images, but spot color/highlight color, and maybe even process color are legal. Here are the kinds of things you need to be looking for.

As much as we've emphasized the graphic files formats, remember that in many cases it is going to be easier to just re-create the graphic using new tools. You still have to know the dimensions and other physical characteristics of the graphic, and be able to manipulate it in the final file, so lists of what you have and what created them will be very helpful.

Challenges and Solutions

Why don't your graphics, which were created for your 240, 480, 300, or 600 dpi print devices, look right on the screen? There are many possibilities, but start with problem identification and work through the steps.

1. Does the image appear to be the wrong size with relation to the text around it as they all appeared in print?

    If so, you may have a problem in the program handling the conversion or in some parameters that you are feeding it. If you are building the document from the ground up, perhaps you selected an incorrect size parameter when you converted your page segment, IOCA, GOCA, LGO or IMG file to the appropriate GIF file.

2. Did the image pick up a *moiré* pattern or become *pixelated*?

   If so, look again to the transform program and its parameters if you are using one. Also look carefully at the original image. If it is an exceptionally complex image with many shades of gray, you may not be able to cleanly reflect it in the 72 dpi world of the web. Seriously consider remaking your graphics. If you are in a production environment, consider have a separate library for the transform program to look at that uses a less complex form of the image.

3. Does the image turn into a blob?

   That's the technical way of expressing the problem associated with complex images (again!) not having enough dots to resolve into on the screen. If you notice that the screen version of an image clumps up like cat litter, look to the solutions above.

4. Are the colors different?

   The fact is that they will usually be different. Remember that we work with about 217 colors in the ideal web world. In the color toner world, we work with mixes of red, green, blue and black that are treated differently and have different chemical elements than those in the phosphorous of the screen. This is one of those places where you have to look carefully at your motivations. Is a specific shade a requirement because some art director says so, or for some more legitimate reason? (Apologies to the sane art directors in the crowd.)

This is the time where you need to stand back and ask if getting a good, clean, crisp image is better than trying to work miracles since every monitor treats the signals for red, green, and blue a bit differently, and even a change in the video card can change what you see. For most business documents, moving to nice spot colors with lower resolution images is more effective at communication than pixel-shy attempts at high-resolution images.

The rule of thumb is going to be to keep the image sizes as small as possible to keep load times effective, and to take a good look during your testing to ensure that what you see on the screen is what you expect. If worse comes to worse and you cannot come up with a good, transformed version of a graphic, consider remaking the graphic with a web-friendly tool, then running it through a product like Adobe's ImageReady (now a feature of Adobe Photoshop) to ensure that you have an optimized image, and talk with your web folks about just-in-time image substitution.

Some final thoughts

In addition to the issues surrounding the format of the graphics, there are issues surrounding how the graphic is called in the original print stream and how it is positioned in the file. Sometimes the graphics formatted relative to "print" records so that if record ends are lost the graphics may be destroyed. This problem arises when transform programs are used and the files are moved between systems and platforms. It helps to have a print of the original data stream in its original environment to compare with so that you can tell if you drop graphics or if they appear in a different location.

Remember that the AFP List and Xerox List hosted by Xplor are great sources of help if you encounter problems that seems to escape solution.

Forms/Overlays

Round 10

One of the easiest resources to overlook is the electronic forms overlay. Even though it may be one of the most common resources, it seems to disappear, so as the inventory of resources is built take special care to locate all of the forms in use.

> Forms can be inline or referenced, and may be anything from a simple page border to a complex legal disclosure.

> Forms can have their own font and graphic issues, so be on the lookout for logo variations and custom fonts not used elsewhere in the print environment.

There may also be pre-printed forms still in the print mix. Take care not to confuse pre-printed forms with electronic forms.

You are almost ready to put the whole thing together, but before you do there is one last object to review. Electronic overlays, forms, form overlays, electronic forms, or whatever you want to call them. They are generally stored as files, either in a designated directory or on the printer, which are often the equivalent of pre-printed forms, though at times there are both preprints and electronic forms involved in the same print job. Part of the trick in

getting to the web and beyond is making sure that you don't
lose them along the way!

This does mean yet another extension to the catalogue of
lists, and this one could get complicated. Our concerns
include vendor-specific file formats and the systems that
might have created those forms.

In an IBM environment, printing to IBM, Océ, MPI/i-data,
Lexmark, or even Xerox AFP printers, your electronic
form is called an Overlay. The overlay is a special file
format defined in the AFP architecture. The overlays are
referenced in the print job so that one copy is stored and
they are repeated for each page as defined in the print job.
An overlay can contain text and graphics in any of the
available AFP formats. The fonts and graphics that appear
in the overlay may not be used anywhere else in your
print environment. It's also common to find forms that
contain text blocks that are really graphics, either to use
a special font not available on the printer or to make the
text significantly smaller than the type sizes available. As
you look at the overlays, review them for these types of
anomalies.

Also, watch for the orientation of the overlays. In an AFP
environment, the overlays can be portrait or landscape,
and within the print job you may also see some that are
upside down. If you have ever looked at a legal contract or
insurance policy you might notice that many are bound at
the top so that if you lift the page the text is technically
upside down on the page, but you can read it because of
the way the page appears to you when you lift it. That
is accomplished in business printing by a technique called
tumble-duplex. Remember that if you have overlays that are
stored upside down in your library, you will have a few
challenges getting them displayed in a usable manner on a
screen.

AFP Overlays are usually identifiable in PC environments by
the extension OVY or OVL. In MVS and VM environments,
you will usually see an extension or filetype of OVERLAY.
They are usually found in a dedicated library (directory),
and there may be more than one. You may find a single
production library, or you may find that the file system

has been set up so that each product you print draws from a separate overlay library, just as with your fonts and graphics. Don't be surprised to find that some of the overlays in production reside in a test or QA directory, and the version in the production library is out of date. It happens all of the time. Notice that we haven't talked about what created them yet. We'll get back to that.

In the Xerox printing environment, using LCDS devices to print DJDE and line data or Metacode print files, we have electronic forms, often called an FRM. This comes from the extension you find them under on the Xerox printer's hard drive. FRMs are specially-formatted files that are usually called by reference in the print job. As in the AFP world, the FRMs contain fonts and graphics, some of which may be unique to the FRM environment. And we also have the use of the tumble-duplex technique to accomplish insurance and legal printing. All of the same concerns apply. Identify any of the unusual features of your electronic forms as you make your list.

So, we have AFP Overlays and/or Xerox FRMs for electronic overlays. Either one may be composed of text only, text and image, or image only. In that last case, you might see a full-page raster image wrapped with the code to identify it as an electronic overlay. This is an important distinction since the text in the image may not come through a transform to a web format and still be readable. There is a huge difference between the resolution of text in an image at 240 dpi or 300 dpi on a high-speed printer, and the screen resolution. Make sure you identify any of these types of electronic overlays and label them as potential problems.

Now take a look at what might have created those electronic forms. If they are older, they were probably created used a command-driven language. In the AFP world, you might have used the Overlay Generation Language (OGL).

In the Xerox world, you might have used the Forms Description Language (FDL) on the Xerox printer or the Host Forms Description Language (HFDL) on an IBM mainframe to create and compile the electronic forms. In this case, the development was a trial and error process. You put commands into a file with coordinates to draw lines and boxes, placed the text and graphics and ran a program to generate the electronic form format. Then you had to print it to see if it was correct. Not efficient, but it was the only way available. If this is how your forms were developed, be sure that the forms you make available for the move to the new output environment are the production versions and not the test versions.

Then came the dawn of third party vendor solutions, and we began to see more forms design workstations. Older equipment like the Intran and Tyrego systems with dedicated workstations and special monitor cards gave way to PC-based systems like Elixir, Isis, and others. If you use a forms development workstation that is on a PC platform, be sure that the forms you move into the web process are the real production forms and not something sitting in a test or development directory. The good news is that most of the forms developed on the PC will use fonts that will be web-friendly.

That takes care of the electronic forms, but you may also have pre-printed stock. You will need to take a careful look at what you print and find out what, if any, pre-printed stock is used and if it is an integral part of what you need to display. Often there are large blocks of text in the pre-printed form that you must reproduce to provide a valid display version. If this is the case, find out who created the masters and their format. Make another list, check it twice.

A Question of Migration & Fidelity

Round 11

Moving output to a new delivery environment is sometimes the easiest part of the project. Sometimes the hardest is the subjective issue of how the output looks in the new environment. Here is where you need to make the tough decisions.

> Do you create a perfect copy of the paper, or do you re-design to ensure usability in your new environment?
>
> Can you re-purpose the information or must you re-deliver the information?
>
> Who can make the decisions if something has to change?

Look at all of your technical options, but remember that there are business issues, too.

If you don't know how, where, and by whom your printer environment was established, you reduce your chances of successfully moving that data to the web or other alternative delivery environment. The more you know about how the data is currently configured, generated, and managed, the better your odds are of working around the anomalies in the data that you will inevitably find during your project.

How you create your data, and how you route it to your printers and archive systems today will determine how you approach the alternative print devices, as well as other delivery devices. Some of what you learn may surprise you, but remember that each application was acquired or created to meet a specific business need at a specific point in the enterprise history. The resources available and the prevailing state of the technology were primary considerations.

By now you know that you will need to look at the applications that create the print , as well as the makes and models of the printers currently in use. You need not only the make and model information, but also the information about when your organization put the hardware into service and what the firmware support levels are for each printer and its supporting environment.

You may learn that you have applications that only print on one specific device. Or, you may learn that you are maintaining older printers because the applications that print on them were never migrated. If you are very lucky, you may find that all of your files will print on any printer owned by the enterprise, but that is a rare case.

For each of the types of printers and print file formats you use actively, there are fonts, graphics, print control files, electronic forms files, and other print applications files. Who is responsible for these files in the organization? One person? One department? Or, does each functional department have responsibility for their own files. Who can update resources and add new resources? Who makes the decisions about what is an acceptable image and what fonts are acceptable? This is critical information since you will need to work with the owners of the print resources to understand what they have and what their requirements are.

Remember that files created 15 or 20 years ago have different characteristics than files created 10 years ago, 5 years ago or last week. The supporting resources have also evolved. Who knows how to modify and maintain the oldest resources?

Pareto Principle: The 80:20 Rule

You may have heard of the 80:20 Rule, also known as the Pareto Principle. You see it cited in most business texts as a rule-of-thumb for determining when the effort you put into a project or resource outstrips the value you will see in return. It's based on the work of Italian economist Vilfredo Pareto, who practiced his trade in the late 19th century. He started by identifying that 80% of the land in Italy was owned by 20% of the population. An interesting proposition, but not the basis for a theory. Then, as he was gardening, he noticed that 20% of the peapods produced 80% of the pea harvest. After some refinement, a theory was born and it is still in use today.

Applied to Migration the theory let's us know that 80% of your problems will come from just 20% of your documents!

The most common method of making legacy data available on the web is to put it through some type of transform program to convert it to HTML, XML, PDF, or, rarely, an image format. The good news is that there are many products and vendors to choose from, and most are tested in the trenches. The bad news is that they are not usually configured to handle the addition of pre-printed overlays, though they generally handle electronic overlays. Keep this in the back of your mind as you start looking at your real requirements for moving your legacy files to the web.

Even if you do everything right, the results of moving to a new output platform may not look like that nice form that your offset print shop always printed for you, or those FRMs or overlays your forms coding department crafted over the past 10 years. Why not? If you do everything correctly, and follow all of the rules, why the disappointment?

The problem is that your legacy data, no matter how diligently you understand it, was made for 240 or 300 dpi laser print devices, and as you know, that screen you are trying to display that data on is a few pixels short on the resolution. So what do you do?

The basic question is, "How important is it for the print and web versions to look identical?" What about the document as a whole? The overall document will tend to pick up some formatting inconsistencies as they come through any transformation. These is true whether you use a transformation program that reads in your print datastream and converts it to PDF or HTML, or you strip down to the bare text and regenerate the HTML, XML, or XHTML (let alone HML or WML).

This is a big question in many industries. In the insurance and financial industries used to be taken as gospel that the displayed image must be identical to the printed image delivered via the post office. In any industry, the advertising department will sing a song of color wheels and the requirements for specific shades of blue and red to convey their marketing messages. And many managers, not knowing what the research says about comprehension of documents on the web or readability and usability of documents on the web, will insist that the documents be made "light table" identical. Imagine holding up the paper to your screen and having to make everything identical. It's a tough job. Especially when you understand that screens come in many resolutions and configurations, which can change the way colors are displayed and fonts are rendered.

If the original formatting is very tight (edge-to-edge) it may be impossible to render the document accurately in a new medium. Look at how the original available page real estate was consumed. How much real estate does the new environment permit? These are all serious considerations.

To Migrate or Not To Migrate

Not every document in your organization is a candidate for dispersal beyond the printed page. Blasphemous as that may sound at this point, it's true. In fact, a review of the documents catalogued and maintained by your company may uncover many documents that no longer have any use, but remain in the catalogues as available because someday they might be needed. A bit of common sense applies here. If you have a dense form that is used to request Telex transmissions, but your company has moved forward and no longer uses the Telex machine, don't migrate the form!

Some of this may seem a bit simplistic, but a look at an average company will show that you can eliminate at least 20 percent of the internal documents on the company's books. Many are redundant, and many have become obsolete with the introduction of new technology. If we apply a variation of the Pareto Principal (see the sidebar), we'd go so far as to say that only 20 percent of the documents are used to conduct 80 per cent of the business. That leaves a lot of room for critical review.

So, the first rule is to be sure that the documents you want to move to a web-enabled or alternative delivery environment really belong there.

The next concern is more legal than graphic. Many documents in many industries must meet some government or industry requirement to be considered in compliance for official information distribution. For example, OSHA, the FDA, and others have strict formatting requirements for the paper versions of the documents they regulate the use of. Things like Material Safety Data Sheets (MSDS) must meet rigorous requirements for formatting, legibility and readability. To move regulated documents to a web-enabled delivery environment requires careful consultation with the regulators to ensure that you do not spend time and money creating a document that they will not permit you to use.

The next point of inquiry concerns the use of the document. Is it one that has *fill-in-the-blank* spaces or does it simply provide information. The design issues are different for each type of document. For forms that require interaction, where the ultimate output is to paper, the information collection screen on the web does not have to be the same as the paper version of the form. For a variety of reasons you might want it to be, but in a strictly technical sense you can collect data and reformat it on the way to the printer, even in a web-enabled environment. If you choose this route you must still ensure that the reader has the same access to any instructional information available on the printed version of the form, but this can be done with rollover tips, instructional pop-up windows, and other techniques.

There are volumes written to describe the best way to format web documents created for the purpose of data collection. Some advocate *chunking* the input fields into small groups with continuations at the bottom of each screen. They advocate keeping the screens to a single panel without the requirement to scroll down. But, there is ample evidence to indicate that users of web applications do not require the hand-holding that such a design requires. Companies like the User Interface Engineering group, under Jared Spool's leadership, have been demonstrating that users tend to work more quickly and accurately on long forms without breaks.

Remember the basics, though. Give users enough room to enter the information you ask for. Constraining fields by length or types of characters should be avoided whenever possible. Use color to indicate required fields. Use strong typography so that the text is easy to read and follow. Avoid extraneous lines and boxes unless they add value to the data gathering process.

For documents that are for information only, go back to the tips and techniques you can find on dozens of web sites about usability, color, density, and typography to re-flow the documents for ease of use. If your organization still has people using older monitors with lower resolution, be kind and test any documents you reformat to ensure that they can be seen on the oldest and newest of the monitors in use. If some of the documents or forms will be accessed from handheld computers or PDAs, test on those, too. Remember, your company may have purchased the PCs over time, so video drivers and video memory available may vary throughout the organization. Keep the pages simple, easy to read, and easy to navigate whenever you have control.

Reformatting When Necessary

There are documents that you will want to migrate that may require reformatting to make the move. Documents that were tightly formatted for specific print environments may become unreadable when migrated to lower resolution output devices.

You will know them when you see them. They will be documents that appear too tight or too widely spaced. Fixed line lengths may be inappropriate for the new devices. Tables may become unintelligible.

Before you head to the design shop, do a bit of investigation into who really owns the original document and who will own the document in its new environment. If it becomes necessary to reformat, you will need their input and approval.

As you evaluate the documents, give careful thought to the original page orientation and page size of the documents. Page orientation and proportions are generally different than a screen of any dimension. You can test it for yourself. Take a standard letter size or A4 piece of paper and hold it up to your cell phone screen or your PC screen. Even if you hold it in landscape orientation, it's not an exact fit.

Another area of concern is the use of color. Spot and highlight color have become more common in the last 5 years. Consultants to the print industry demonstrated that a little bit of color went a long way to getting people to pay their bills faster and to retain messages in all manner of documents.

Remember, however, that the color that prints to a laser or inkjet printer has different characteristics than those of a screen. The color screen has only a static red, static green, and static blue available to resolve color. That means that a color that may have been achieved on paper will usually look different when viewed on a screen. It should not invalidate the use of color, but it is something to be prepared for.

Now that you know what you have… what do you want?

The time has come to make use of all of those lists you've been building and make some decisions. If you've been following the plan you have made lists of all of your document types and what creates them, where they print, and what graphics they use. You've made corollary lists of electronic overlays (forms), and taken a hard look at what created your graphics. You've also given some serious thought to your font situation.

The time for meditation is over. Now it's time to do something. That first *something* is to pick a project and migrate it.

There are any number of places you might start, but let's begin with some plain line data. Every business has some. You may have either EBCDIC (IBM mainframe) line data or ASCII (PC, UNIX, some mainframe applications) line data, or both. It is most often created by COBOL programs written any time over the past twenty-five years, often under a deadline and without regard to issues like re-usability. When line data isn't created by a COBOL program, the source can be almost anything, including programs purchased from vendors, shareware, and programs created in C, PASCAL, FORTRAN, and Assembler (to name just a few languages). Regardless of what creates it, line data can be the hardest thing you move to the web even though it looks so simple when it prints.

Just as a refresher, line data was originally designed to print on line printers. Those are the print devices that look or behave like very fast typewriters. These are often found on shop floors, in back offices, or in the IT print room churning out boxes of print each day. They may use print chains or moving balls, but what they have in common is that the data that is passed to them includes control characters to tell them when to advance the paper, when to overprint to create bold type, and even when to change type faces on printers that support it. As we discussed in earlier chapters, line print can also be fed to almost any printer Xerox DJDE/ Metacode printers, AFP printers from a variety of vendors, and most other printers as long as the proper commands precede the data. Industry estimates still indicate that most printing done today is conditioned for line printers even though it may be heading for a more sophisticated device.

Line Data Tips

Look at the formatting:

- CC, TRC
- LRECL

Font: Fixed or Proportional

Can the application producing the print be altered to use standard fonts?

Is the data printed edge-to-edge?

Can you reformat it from the application?

The line data you want to move to the web is probably in a report format. In many companies these are the reports that are run each evening so that they can be distributed to the analysts before dawn each morning. The common candidates are internal accounting reports, work-in-progress reports, wellhead reports, shipping reports, transaction reports and other statistical reports that provide status information to a wide audience. Now you will stop the printing and make the information available via an internal web page for everyone to access as they need it.

The first thing to do is to analyze the line data to determine how it is composed. Does it have carriage control, line feeds or font index bytes. Is it a fixed record format, where every line is the same length (even if that means it's padded with blanks), or is it a variable format where every line is a different length? What is the maximum record or line length? Is it ASCII or EBCDIC? These are the easy questions.

Now for the challenge. What do you want this information to look like once you get it to the web? Should it just be an image of the report as it is created, or should it have some bells and whistles added in for usability?

To make this easy, let's start with the basics and just get the pages on to the web. You have several paths, some more sophisticated than others.

You can write a procedure that grabs the report data and routes it to a file, which you then strip of the carriage control and other information so that it is simply lines of text formatted with spaces. If you wrap that file in PRE and end-PRE tags, save it as an HTML file and place that file on a file server accessible to the people who need the information, you will have a web report! Not pretty and not sophisticated, but any browser will be able to pull up the file and the normal FIND option in the browser should be able to find any string you want to locate.

You can write a more sophisticated program that actually adds a bit more HTML into the file. You could set fonts, and maybe even segment the file by the target department or target recipient so that each group only wades through the data they need. The level of programming skill to do this is minimal and the usability is enhanced quite a bit.

You can write a program that invokes the Adobe Acrobat API or a third part PDF-generator to create a PDF (Portable Document Format) file, which can be viewed from a web browser. The advantage to PDF is that a user can annotate the files, which can be helpful in customer service and account analysis operations. The API allows you to designate things like the base font and the page dimensions of the displayed file. With PDF, you can view it with a web browser or natively with the Acrobat viewing program that Adobe makes available for free from their website.

You can buy one of the vendor packages that transforms your data into HTML, PDF, XML or XHTML. One of the advantages of buying a program to do the transformation of your line data is that most of the vendors who sell in this space have vast experience in line data and have written their code to handle the variations allowed in line data files.

Notice that we added a new wrinkle. Not just HTML, but PDF, XML, and XHTML are viable output formats for you. Why not just produce some HTML and be done with it? There are several things to think about before you make your final decision. The most important is the usability factor. If you move your legacy reports to the web, but they are hard to read and hard to navigate, your users will resort to printing them and you will have lost the advantage you gained by going online. Remember that it is significantly more costly for your users to demand print to a convenience printer than it is for you to cause batch printing to high-speed devices, even when you factor in the delivery costs. The significant cost savings occurs when users don't feel that they need paper to do their job since everything they need is easily available and usable online.

Where do you look for these packages? Start with the vendors you already work with. Many of the companies that you work with to meet your printing needs today can help you locate vendors who will understand your data and work with it reliably. Xerox, IBM, Océ, Lexmark, as well as the enterprise groups at Computer Associates, Xenos, Anacomp, Pitney Bowes, and others can help you navigate the set up and production requirements. Remember that regardless of how you choose to do it, you'll need all of those lists we started with.

If the legacy data you are working with is flat, line data generated by an in-house or commercial system, it may be formatted by an external device. Not a physical device, but a virtual device or filter that conditions the data for the target printing device. The big question as you approach the web with your data is what you want it to look like when it appears on the screen. As we asked earlier, must it be a mirror of the document as it prints or should it be more web-friendly?

This is the first question that should be answered but often the last question that *is* answered. It is important because it should direct how you approach the data and applications you are using today. If your goal is to use the web-enabled version of your documents as little more than an archive, by all means make the documents look identical to the paper documents. Here are some sample scenarios where this is your best option:

- Documents used in support of a call center. For example, banks and insurance companies who send out policies, statements, and other supporting documents often rely on green-screen data views instead of the image of the actual documents in the customer's hands.

  When the customer says, "The third line down on page four has an error," the call center operator is at a loss to know what the called is really seeing.

- Documents sent to customers. Invoices, billing statements, or catalogs and price lists. If the formatting of the information is integral to the exchange of information and it is likely to be viewed on paper as well as on a screen, keeping the look and feel identical is the best route.

- Documents that are graphically rich and rely on the formatting. This might be a catalog or direct mail piece used to stimulate sales as part of an advertising campaign, but it could also be a user guide or maintenance manual.

  First reports of incidents in the insurance industry often meet this criteria when they include photographs and diagrams. Real Estate offers are another candidate.

These are not all of the possibilities, but you should see the pattern. When there are multiple target users of a document, separated by time and space, who must potentially confer about the information contained in the document, preserving the fidelity of the original document is a pretty good idea. There is a caveat in this. If the original documents are formatted edge-to-edge in small fonts with little white space, they are not a candidate for moving to the web in the current format. They are candidates for re-design before the adventure of moving to the web even starts!

On the opposite side of the fence are those documents which would benefit from serious reformatting to make them usable online. Documents that have a wide variety of fonts and font sizes, tabular material formatted for landscape presentation, and highly blocked formatting make documents almost unusable if moved online without serious re-design. Think of some of the common business documents, such as applications, audit forms, and surveys that are built in two-column format. Displaying such formatted texts on the screen in two-column format makes them hard to read and hard to use.

So, we have set up a conundrum. We want to keep documents that have multiple users who must confer about them in as close to the original format as we can, but we do not want to mimic documents on the web in such a way that they are hard to use or worse, unreadable. This takes a bit of planning, which should start with a task force to identify the documents that are targets for a migration to web delivery.

You'll want to separate your documents into two basic categories:

- Documents that must be mirror images on paper and screen

- Documents that should be reformatted before being used for display

For the moment, let's concentrate on the documents that must remain identical.

Once you have your categories, look critically at your documents and assign them to a bucket. For those documents that must be identical in all presentations, look for potential problem areas such as custom fonts, multi-column presentation, tabular data, and overly large or small fonts. Look carefully at the footers and document identification information, which is often produced in 4- or

5-point type. Remember that when you move to the web you are moving from an 8.5 x 11 (US Letter) or 210mm x 297mm (A4) environment to a presentation environment that you have little control over. For some users the screen is in 640 x 480 pixel mode, while for others it will be in 1024 x 768 or greater. There are higher and lower resolutions, and even the video card in the individual machine can change what a viewer sees on the screen. Colors will vary by screen and video driver, and fonts available for display will vary with the individual installation unless you take some drastic action to ensure font availability for your documents.

It is as big a job as it sounds like. You do have several paths to that mirror image. You can create an HTML/DHTML/XML version that formats the data and controls formatting through a style file, you can convert to PDF, or you can convert to image. The easiest is often to convert to image since for most environments this often takes little more than putting a fax driver into the output environment and then wrapping the bitmap as a GIF or PNG file. The downside is that this tends to produce very large files that are not searchable and take forever to load to the screen. It's fast to develop and very slow to use. But it can be a short-term solution. To be usable, it needs a file indexing methodology and an architecture to provide a path to the required documents in some logical manner, but it can be done.

Considering XML

You can find books on XML in every bookstore you walk into, so we'll refer you to any of the many XML books, sites like XML.COM, and the World Wide Web Consortium (www.w3c.org) for all of the information you could want, and more. Some of the basics help, though.

XML and HTML share a common parent in the Standard Generalized Markup Language (SGML), which became ISO Standard 8879. SGML defines the rules for creating sets of tags that define the structure of a document. As envisioned, SGML was to be the basis for the creation of industry-specific and application-specific tag sets that permitted documents to become data interchange mechanisms. The problem with SGML was that it became too cumbersome. Within the SGML family of standards was an alphabet soup of corollary standards for specification of all types of information. There was DSSSL to specify the semantics of the tag set, and FOSI to identify the formatting characteristics of a document. Only a few industries adopted standard Document Type Definitions (DTDs), the backbone of creating SGML-compliant documents, and most of those were confined to the definition of technical documentation.

HTML, the Hypertext Markup Language, grew from the SGML initiative. It adopted the SGML concept of a hierarchical tagging language, but relied on the Web Browsers or other parser technology to interpret the tags into a formatted document, usually a web page. As far as it goes HTML provides a structured way to identify document elements for consistent interpretation. Of course, HTML does not always look the same in to every web browser, but the rules for tagging are well documented and if you violate the rules your results may not be consistent across all browser environments.

Another breakdown in the concept is that there is not an easy way to extend HTML to identify industry-specific or application-specific constructs, such as First Name, Last Name, Address, Bill Amount, Payment Amount, Routing Code, or other fields commonly found in business interchange. Even the document elements were often treated to long strings of attributes to alter global definitions for Heading Level 1 formatting, paragraph formatting and formatting of other page elements.

The initial attempts to wedge meta-information into HTML pages led to a number of industry-specific initiatives, many that began by adding structured comment records and browser add-ons to filter the information adequately.

From that beginning. HTML was expanded, but could never meet the requirements of data interchange for business-to-business or business-to-consumer transactions. XML rose to fill the need by providing a specification for defining tags and making their definitions available to web browsers and application programs. The core structure of an XML application is the DTD or schema that defines what tags are available and how they relate to one another.

XML is codified in the XML Specification managed by the W3C. The specification provides the core requirements for an XML-compliant application, such as what structures are legal. XML supports a growing number of optional specifications and guidelines for specific tasks in the XML environment, such as:

- Xlink: specification for coding consistent hyperlinks
- XPointer and XFragments for pointing to parts of an XML document
- CSS (Cascading Style Sheets), the style sheet language created for HTML
- XSL (Extensible Style Language) the advanced language for expressing style sheets
- XSLT, a transformation language that is often useful for rearranging, adding or deleting tags & attributes is a recommendation
- DOM (Document Object Model) is a standard set of function calls for manipulating XML (and HTML) files from a programming language
- XML Namespaces is a specification that describes how you can associate a URL with every single tag and attribute in an XML document. What that URL is used for is up to the application that reads the URL, though. RDF (Resource Definition Framework), W3C's standard for metadata
- XML Schemas 1 and 2 to define XML-based formats
- XML/EDI for using XML applications to replace EDI transactions
- XHTML, the reformulation of HTML as an XML 1.0 specification is a working draft
- XQL, XML Query LanguageXPath, XML Path language 1.0 is a recommendation
- Xinclude: the general purpose inclusion specification for ML-compliant and non-compliant documents
- Xforms: the standard for passing data from web forms via XML protocols.

There are others that have been offered to the W3C for consideration, too. The normal process is for a company, consortium or other entity to offer a specification or API for consideration to the W3C. The W3C announces the availability and releases a Call for Comment with a deadline. After all of the comment is received the proposal may be set out for a vote or sent to a committee for further action. The end result of the process may be a new specification, or simply a set of guidelines..

Many of the applications you use today use or are compatible with XML. Some use Document Type Definitions and others use schemas to define the XML tags used in the data files for managing and exchanging, and displaying the information. It is worth checking to see if there is an XML specification common to your industry that might work in your environment. Check internal sources and check with your vendors.

XML documents can configure themselves to match the characteristics required by the display device. Another benefit is that XML markup also turns documents into intelligent, searchable databases, providing the ability to turn documents lively and interactive when needed, or static and to the point when needed.

XML was designed to allow you to do whatever you need to do to tag the data for multiple uses, and to apply formatting information as a sidebar function that can be mapped to specific output environments. Of course, if you want to play in the world of wireless connectivity, display on other wired devices, and still print and view as needed, you need to have a few standards to play by. If you tag your invoices with the tag <CUSTNO> for customer number, but other members of the billing consortium use <CUSTOMERNUM>, you are going to have a problem sharing data. Add to that simple example the whole range of transport protocol information that now lives in XML documents and you begin to get the picture that adopting standard XML tag sets is an important part of the process.

Again, look within your industry (insurance, banking, manufacturing) and learn what XML standards (DTDs and Schemas) are proposed or already in use. Learn what they are and how they are used. You will probably find that there are several XML sets handling different information dissemination issues. Electronic Funds transfers and stock purchase confirmations have different requirements than bills of lading or irrevocable letters of credit.

Considering PDF

If this isn't for you, consider PDF. Adobe's Portable Document Format is viewable through both Netscape and Internet Explorer as long as you are up-to-date on your installation, and is also emerging as the ebook standard. Creating PDF from existing applications can be reasonably easy to do. Check out PDFZone at http://www.pdfzone.com for a truckload of utilities for turning the formats you have into PDF. The downside of PDF is that it is larger than flatter formats like HTML, but the upside is that you get in the PDF view what you saw on paper. You can scale the view on the screen and you can even establish bookmarks and views in the PDF document during its creation to make navigation easier. If you have ever seen a demonstration of the Merrill Lynch customer statement environment you have seen how PDF can be generated automatically by a legacy system to produce an incredibly navigable user experience.

But if only the flattest format will do, then you are down to tagging your data in HTML or XML, with the supporting formatting issues. This can be a difficult task since the fonts available for print are often quite different than those available on the web. How white space is allocated and even how line breaks are calculated is quite different as well. However, if you generate your HTML or XML so that you force the margins and line lengths as well as the page depth (often by using tables and treating each cell as a "page"), you can make it work. There are a few good vendor tools for getting to tagged mark-up while preserving the look and feel of a print version, so interrogate all of your vendors and take a close look at XML.com. Quite a few vendors have built transforms or work with transform vendors to provide a solution when this is the route you want to take.

What AFP Looks Like

In Hex:

```
CHAR ! Lyy   AFP
ZONE 501DAAOOOCCD44444
NUMR A0038800216700000
   O1...5...10...15..
CHAR 1 Ly   1
ZONE 501DAAOOOF4444444
NUMR A0038F00110000000
   O1...5...10...15..
```

Remember to ask questions about how they will guarantee the formatting, and be prepared to make some decisions about handling custom fonts and proprietary fonts which may not be available any place on the web.

So, pick a preparation method and try it. Review the output and find the holes, including missing formatting and characters for formatting that overruns its boundaries. Remember to review how the formatting controls were handled. Make sure that all of the special characters appear as needed. Look for telltale DJDE or X'5a controls that might have been embedded directly into the data by an application or places where a post-processor may have called electronic forms, font changes, or page ejects. Were they honored?

If the original application used programmatic bursters or collators, were those actions honored correctly? Does it make sense to write alternative post-processors, or new post-processors to re-condition the data? Or, have new products come on the market to do the job more efficiently?

Stepping up to Complex Data

Moving line data to a new environment can be extremely difficult because so little of the format information is in the print file. Moving more complex data is equally tricky because the format information *is* in the print file. Of course, it might be both inside and outside of the print file, too. Regardless of which type of complex data format you start with, the migration or transform will be a challenge.

The basic issues faced in moving line data also apply to moving complex data, so think carefully about the application. A complex, custom application using tight formatting and custom fonts will pose much more of a challenge than flat text output from an industry standard text formatting application. Are you prepared for all of the challenges?

As with all adventures in technology, there will be several paths you can take. Look over the information we give you, and then have a serious chat with all of the people in your organization to see what path is most appropriate.

A Sample AFP Migration Plan

In the IBM world, you find line data, line data conditioned with Advanced Function Printing (AFP) Page Definitions (PageDefs) and Form Definitions (FormDefs), plus the true composed AFP datastream and its variations produced by ACIF (a packaging tool for archiving AFP datastreams). Let's not forget that many vendors have products that produce AFP print steams, and quite a few vendors manufacture AFP printers. This means that there may be variations in the AFP datastream depending on what your normally targeted printer is.

If you have line data files that are conditioned with PageDefs and FormDefs, which is the vast majority of all AFP printing today, you have to ensure that the fonts, graphics, overlays, and conditions programmed into the PageDef page formats and FormDef copy groups are handled appropriately for your output to the web. The fonts are a straightforward issue, by now. If you've read the earlier chapters, you know to look for what fonts are used in your applications and what options you have to mirror them on the web.

For most line data in an IBM print environment, the fonts have no default equivalent in the web world. This is where the hard decisions come into play. If you must have and exact duplicate you may be forced to burn your print file to an image format and display the image. Messy and bandwidth consuming at best; hard to read for most of us as well. If you have more flexibility, try selecting something like Courier or the MS Terminal font and see how that works for your application.

All of the processing that handles overlays, and the programming in PageDefs and FormDefs, must be handled by some process to move the print file to the web. If you have skilled programmers you may be able to handle the problem in-house by writing small programs to re-process the file instead of feeding it through the process that now creates the AFP print file. This takes extremely in-depth knowledge of both AFP and the underlying architecture. Both PageDefs and FormDefs can alter how the data is placed in the output page, as well as controlling the overlay calls and the pagination.

It may not seem like a lot of work, but there is a tremendous amount of programming behind these tasks. Consider things like conditional processing that reads triggers in the datastream, and pagination that is intelligent about simplex and duplex printing. And don't forget orientation issues. If you have a PageDef/FormDef combination that allows for tumble/duplex printing (every other page is upside down), what happens when you put that on the web?

If your target application was written in-house, the more common way of getting to the web is to acquire one of the many transform products that can handle the datastream accurately and allow you to tune the output for the web without touching the original program. If you are using a vendor program to produce your print, start by asking if that vendor has a filter or plug-in that provides a transform inside their existing program environment.

The same rules apply to the composed form of AFP. Check with your vendors first, and if they cannot help, check with the transform vendors to see what they have to offer. Remind them of the font issues you face and the needs you have with regard to your graphics. There are big resolution differences for the graphics to contend with, so you need to be prepared for some compromises. This is now a mature industry and there are many options available. Those lists you made will help you discuss your needs and current print file specifications with your vendors so that they can give you ideas of what they have to offer.

Remember that whether you do it yourself or rely on vendor programs, testing will be critical. Allow twice the amount of time you think you will need to do the testing; the odds are you will use it.

A Sample Xerox Migration Plan

If you are in a Xerox environment, your printers may print line data, line data conditioned with DJDEs, or Metacode. As in the IBM world, line data is still the most common print format, and line data conditioned with DJDEs (Dynamic Job Descriptor Entries) is found around the world. There are tremendous variations in how DJDEs are programmed and consequently, a huge difference in how print files may behave when put through transform processes. When line data and DJDEs are combined with Metacode in print files, as they often are, the complexity involved in moving the data to the web is immense, but it can be done successfully.

First, you have the font issues to contend with. As always, if you are using the ubiquitous P0612b or P06BOB fonts, you have the challenge of finding fonts that will do the trick for you. This is going to be tough, but you have several options. Font vendors like Terrapin and ASE (see Appendix C for contact information) sell Windows-friendly versions of the full Xerox font set and this may do the trick for you. Remember that if you rely on them you will need to ensure that those same fonts will be available to the browser of everyone who needs to see the pages that use the font.

And you'll have the graphics to contend with. Remember that the file formats are quite different and there is always the chance that the web version of a graphic may not be what you had hoped. Add to the fun the fact that Xerox resources generally reside on the printer, where the programs and transforms can't get access to them. This means mirroring the printer's hard drives on a hard drive that the programs you write or buy can see. Remember this as you begin configuring your environment.

Then you have to decide how to best get to the web with your Xerox files. As in the IBM world you may choose to write your own transform. In the complex world of the Xerox print stream you will need an expert to get you through the process, line data can move to the web with an intervention from a proc or exec with fair success. Metacode is another story, though. It is a proprietary datastream owned by Xerox and therefore documentation on its nuances is hard to come by.

We recommend a close look at the vendors who operate in this niche in the market since they've fought long and hard to develop solutions that will work in a production environment. Companies like Xenos, Elixir, Emtex, Exstream, and ePage(SysPrint) have long histories in dealing with the guts of the high-speed printer datastreams. IBM and Xerox, as well as Océ and MPI/i-data, have groups in their organization who can help with the issues surrounding getting to the web as well.

Remember that if you go the transform route, the transform has to know everything the printer knows. This is a big job. That's what all of the lists are for, and this is why you need your systems folks to tell you how the current printing environment is configured.

That configuration includes the control software, which is the operating system on a Xerox printer, but something like PSF (Print Services Facility) software in an AFP

environment. Note the phrase "something like"; there are
a number of variations on PSF within the IBM world, plus
comparable products from Emtex and Océ.

Suggestions

As the proud owner of legacy data you know that many
of your corporate documents will require re-design and
re-formatting to make them most useful beyond the printed
page. For the short term you can undertake the big project
to fix everything you have all at once, or you could choose
to live with what you have and disregard the usability
issues. Big projects are hard to fund, however, and some
mission critical documents probably deserve immediate
attention. So, the best path is to try a little of both until you
can re-deploy new documents using good design principals.

- Look carefully at your applications during the next
  update cycle and see if you can do a fast font swap in
  the application or its control file.

- Save up a requirements list so that the next time the
  application comes up for maintenance or rewrite your
  requirements are considered.

- Make sure that the departmental design teams and
  other document owners know what your plans are
  so that they can be on the lookout for fast paths to
  getting documents updated and ready for a migration.

- Talk to your printer experts and see if application
  of a new PageDef, FormDef, or JDL would allow a
  quick format update without adversely affecting the
  production print. Caution them to be conservative
  in their creativity, however. Remember that some of
  the problems you are trying to solve were caused by
  creative print programming!

Technology is not standing still, so you will probably see at
least one or two more major migrations during your career.

To stay on top of things, stay up-to-date with your printers and viewing environments. If your company acquires other companies or if you are acquired, get on board with the additional print environment as quickly as possible.

Another safety net is to keep your staff trained in all of the technology you work with. If you don't embark on a consistent education plan, the next migration will be as challenging as the first. Side-by-side with the education requirement should be a plan to review the document area every six months against industry trends and emerging technologies.

Side Thoughts:
Getting to Digital from Paper

We've been concentrating on the idea that you are starting from a disk file, but corporate archives contain millions of pages on paper for which there is no digital original. At some point in the process someone may wonder if it is feasible to consider scanning those pages to make them available online.

The simple answer is yes. Scanning technology has evolved to the point where it is perfectly feasible to consider scanning large volumes of paper files. Remember, though, that the first step in scanning is to capture the image of the page. So far, so good. But, it is only an image and doesn't really embody the information contained in the original document in a searchable form.

It is possible to overlay an index on a scanned image so that a query program can locate the document based on a keyword search. That does require some manual intervention since someone will have to evaluate the document and manually enter the keywords. Again, this is done all of the time and there are vendors who will do it as a fee-based project.

The better solution is to take the process one step farther and do character recognition on the scanned image. The recognition, sometimes called OCR (Optical Character Recognition) or ICR (Intelligent Character Recognition), attempts to recognize each character and turn it into its text equivalent. You can find inexpensive programs to do this to scanned images at any computer store.

The consideration is that, for scans, the original pages are no longer as clean and bright as they were originally, often making the scan and subsequent recognition less than accurate. Some estimates say that an average recognition program makes a mistake once every ten characters. It may not sound like much but consider this sentence:

The quick brown fox jumped over the lazy dog.

Now look at it with a mistake once every ten characters:

The guick brown pox jumpcd over the lazg dog.

You can still make out the meaning, but you wouldn't want to keep it on file as the permanent record of the original sentence.

As we said, however, the technology is getting better and with the right set of tuning parameters and clean originals, even these inexpensive programs have been used to move whole warehouses of files to disk.

Companies like Computerstream Limited (www.computerstream.co.uk) in the UK, ScanTastik, Inc. (www. Scantastik.com) in the US, and others around the world have built businesses scanning sensitive corporate documents, and even not-so-sensitive documents, and guaranteeing the accuracy of the final disk files. Most service bureaus like these can also provide indexing and navigation in the final delivered files. If you have corporate knowledge residing in warehouses where it cannot be easily accessed and used, this is a path worth considering.

What's Coming in the Next Generation?

Round 12

Sometimes it's hard to guess what's coming next in the information delivery game, but we have a few clues. At the end of this chapter, you will too!

Getting to new and strange devices.

WAP and more.

This section is for fun, so sit back and imagine the possibilities.

Has anyone asked you to get your data to a WAP phone? A PDA? A Text Pager? How about a billboard in Times Square or Piccadilly Circus? No? Hold on, it could happen to you!

When we first started talking about moving legacy data to the web, the big issues seemed clear. Trying to move some fairly big data chunks that use proprietary formatting to an output device using lower resolution and some interesting variations in real estate and available color was going to pose a few challenges. We needed a plan for those non-standard fonts and graphics, and a strategy for version control across web and paper. That's not everything, but that's a good chunk. If you've been following along, you should be fairly comfortable with the to-do list. So, now there we have one more consideration.

Alternative output devices. We've alluded to them from the beginning of the book, and teased you with the issues, but now it's time to look at the possibilities. Alternative output devices used to mean the Web, but not anymore. Today when we talk about output to alternative devices, we're talking about delivering information to cell phones, PDAs, netpliances, pagers, and even billboards. Don't be surprised if someone starts mumbling about delivering utility bills to refrigerators. You can do it today with the right environment. Don't be too frightened; you already have the skills to deal with it. You just need a bit more information about the real world of alternative devices and you can help your company make better decisions.

Starting with the basics, information delivery is slowly evolving into a world of tagged information. If you've been around the document delivery world for any length of time you may be familiar with tagging languages used to develop documents, like IBM's Document Composition Facility (DCF) and BookMaster, or the Xerox Integrated Composition System (XICS) and Compuset. These tagging languages were used to identify elements in a document, like a paragraph or a heading. The source of the document was processed with a composition program, similar to a compiler for a programming language, and the result was a composed print file in AFP, Metacode, or some similar format.

When the World Wide Web was being born, the folks at the front of that initiative took the same idea to create HTML, the HyperText Markup Language, to tag things like paragraphs and headings so that the browsers would be able to format them to the screen for easy reading.

More recently, the idea of tagging has expanded beyond documents and started to encompass the whole complement of data variations using XML, as we discussed in an earlier chapter. XML is also a component in initiatives to replace Electronic Data Interchange (EDI) applications, ecommerce applications, and many other industry-specific applications. Everyone from the airline industry to supply chain vendors have XML tag sets available to use to accomplish easy information interchange. It shouldn't be a surprise that even PDF is embracing XML structures in its current release.

One of the things a tagging protocol gives us is the ability to re-profile the information based on environmental factors. One profile can produce appropriate output for high-speed print, while another profile formats for the web. We can even have a profile for cell phones, PDAs, and billboards. One of the first attempts to push information beyond the tethered PC uses a variation of XML called WML, the Wireless Markup Language, to do just that.

Using XML and its variations it's possible to push information to phones and fridges. In Europe, there are already extensive implementations of WAP: Wireless Application Protocol. WAP is the communications protocol that makes it possible to send data to a wireless device and it works through the use of WML.

If you understand markup languages and what they can do you know that the groundwork you laid for getting your legacy information to the web in HTML or some form of XML applies here. The trick is that WML is a slim language. It doesn't have a lot of bandwidth to play with or storage on the output device, so today we don't do graphics and we don't use identified fonts. Nevertheless, we will shortly!

Stepping back for a moment, why would you want to get corporate data to someone's phone or PDA? Good question. Think about a couple of applications:

- Customer service people in the printing area currently see job data on their host-attached or network-attached workstation at their desk. When they are walking through the print shop or away from their desk resolving problems there is no way for them to know what other job statuses are. If that information could appear on a PDA that they carry with them everywhere, it would make them more knowledgeable, able to answer questions faster, and a lot more work could be processed with higher quality.

- Sales representatives live and die by their ability to track work in progress, whether it's a tractor, a drilling rig, a software package or an eCRM implementation. They are often on the go, with limited ability to check email in real time. Pagers work to get their attention, but even two-way text messaging pagers like the RIM Blackberry have real limitations. If they could have all work in progress for their customers available real-time on their PDAs, they could save hours of email downloads and phone tag adventures. Knowledge is power!

We've been using the term WAP and we want to be sure you understand that it is not actually available in most the US here in mid-2001, but it may be coming soon. While you may encounter something called a WAP phone, in the US few WAP gateways use the true WAP standard. Sprint PCS phones used an earlier version that relied on their own gateway and a proprietary transform to their own language for displaying text on their phones. That seems to be changing slowly. AT&T Pocket Cell phones relied on their own gateway to use a form of display that complied with older, less elegant WAP standards. That is changing, too. Slowly, we will get everyone reading from the same game book and we'll be able to drive our data to our portable information devices reliably.

So, what do you need to know about your data to drive it to a WAP or other wireless gateway? You need to know how you want it to be displayed on a small screen. What's important and what's not. For the moment, forget corporate logos and color marketing messages, but keep track of them since the technology will catch up quickly. Concentrate on the meat of the information: purchase order numbers and purchase amounts, invoice numbers and amounts, approval codes, job numbers, and anything else that you'd consider critical information. Then, start to look around for WML templates that might work for your industry. Check out resources like the WAP Forum at www.wapforum.org, and the WAP developer's repository at www.wapulous.com. There is even an Open WAP Project at www.openwap.org and WAP toolkits from Nokia and Ericsson. Ask your vendors if they support WAP output from their existing applications. You might be surprised, many already do!

There are infinite possibilities for how all of this comes together with legacy data. Expect to see your AFP output showing up on your cell phone or text pager or PDA. Expect to see Metacode on billboards.

In the best of all possible worlds when someone comes up to you and says, "I need WAP output," or "I need that AFP report on my PDA every morning," you'll be able to smile because you know what you need to do!

The Dreaded Inventory

Round 13

You've been reading about making lists and checking them twice. Here we want give you some ideas on how the process works to help you to avoid some of the common mistakes.

Learning about your environment

Finding hidden workflows and processes

Meeting the people in your company who feed the print applications.

By the end of this chapter you'll know you aren't alone!

Let's start from the premise that knowing what you have will help immeasurably when the time comes to migrate to new delivery methodologies. It's true whether your target is the web, distributed print, CD ROM/DVD, or a Jumbotron. Everything that you don't know can come back to haunt your plans and even scuttle the project. An inventory uncovers the holes in the current understanding of where font, form and graphic resources are actually created, stored, and managed.

Don't be lulled into a sense of security if you find that a resource inventory already exists. Unless you find evidence that the inventory is a living document, plan for it to be inaccurate. Test its accuracy by trying to locate five or ten of the items.

Why We Make Lists

A number of years ago we worked with a large print vendor to help one of their customers migrate from a Xerox print environment to an AFP print environment. In preparation for the migration, we interviewed the print bureau director and the vendor liaison to gain an understanding of the overall Xerox print environment.

We learned that there were six Xerox printers, an old Tyrego system used for creating custom fonts, an old Intran system still in use for scanned graphics, and a set of file folders that mapped print jobs to specific print resources. All of the printers had hard disks full of resources and there was no master directory to identify what resources on what machine might be obsolete.

Our first task was to identify every production job. That meant making a list of all of the customers, and then within each customer identifying the jobs. For each job we had to identify the fonts, logos, and other graphics and forms, as well as the DJDE identifiers and JSLs used.

According to the lists we had more than 10,000 resource files. The customer worked with us to identify acceptable replacement fonts in the AFP environment, but all of the graphics would have to be converted to AFP Page Segments. We had utilities for converting IMG files to Page Segments, and had to write something to take in the LGO files and turn them into Page Segments.

While the resources were being converted, the vendor took care of creating the appropriate PageDefs and FormDefs to emulate the original Xerox environment. When we delivered the new resources a test of every job was executed. In production only 7200 of the 10,000 resources were actually used, and 500 were missed in the conversion.

No matter how many people we talked to and how many lists we made, there were still 500 resource files that were off the radar screen.

We had a similar experience with a company that was adding CD delivery to an AFP operation. They found all of their fonts, forms, and graphics, including inline resources. They came to an agreement on what font substitutions were acceptable, and arranged to have all of their signature fonts converted to a compatible format. Then the tragedy struck.

At a very early point in their print development, they used the IBM Graphmod technology to create Graphmod 3800 signature fonts. While they could identify the fonts, no source could be found meaning that the signatures had to be re-created. All 200 of them.

These are the types of hurdles you will face, no matter how good your inventory skills are. In earlier chapters we offered some ideas on the lists you will need, but remember that working with legacy data concerns more than just the documents and resources.

Business Environment

Your company probably operates on a yearly budget, with restrictions and guidelines regarding capital expenditures, technology upgrades, and required return on investment when implementing new technology. At the start of wrestling match with your legacy data, here are a few questions to ask.

- Is there a budget for this solution?

   That is, a realistic budget. One that accounts for acquisition of new fonts, graphics, and tools.

- Is the budget for this quarter, this year, or farther out?

When you begin to work with legacy data you are starting down a long and convoluted path. If there is money in this quarter's budget, but none for next year, you could have a problem.

- Is there an evangelist in executive management for this solution? \

  As with any new project, an angel in the executive suite makes the problems that come along easier to solve.

- Who has signoff for this solution?

  This varies depending on your corporate culture and corporate structure. Be sure to know who has final say before you start.

- Is a complete system test in house required?

  At some point you are going to have to run your applications and verify that your information is arriving on the target platforms as desired. How is that going to be accomplished? Who will be involved? Is it on their work plan and in their budget?

- Who is making the decision to move information beyond the printer and why?

  Knowing the motivations can help you find the right kind of help if you hit bottlenecks.

System Environment

While the business issues are important, most of the resources lie in the systems area. A bit of detective work at the outset can help avoid misunderstandings later in the project, so try these questions:

- What platforms are in use today?

  Is all computing done on a System 390 host, or do you have a smorgasbord of computing platforms including PC and UNIX networks, midrange systems, multiple host platforms and operating systems?

- Where can transform programs run if they are the best answer?

  The answer will depend on your current environment and how saturated the platforms in use are.

- What connectivity do you have between platforms and environments?

  Can you move data and applications from platform to platform easily, or does it take the intervention of a Systems Programmer? Find out before you try to move anything, anywhere.

Print Environment

You might have print that falls into any or all of these categories:

- **AFP:** 3820 and newer AFP files (native AFP), line mode data conditioned with PageDefs and FormDefs, and mixed mode data.

- **Metacode and Line/DJDE:** Files intended to print on Model 8700 or newer Xerox printers.

- **XES or UDK:** Files intended to print on a Xerox Decentralized printer, Model 2700 or newer.

- **PCL:** Files intended to print on HP PCL printers.

- **PostScript/PDF**: Files created to print on a PostScript printer or view in Acrobat or comparable PDF viewer.

The most intense inventory questions will surround your AFP, Xerox and PCL environments, so don't forget these questions.

If you have AFP...

What is the nature of the AFP environment?

- Line mode with basic PageDefs/FormDefs

  This is the most common type of file. It contains 3211 line data, may contain carriage control bytes at the start of the records, and may contain TRCs at the start of the records.

- Line mode with complex PageDefs/FormDefs, including When = Change processing

  Another common file type, it contains 3211 line data and may contain carriage control bytes at the start of the records, and may contain TRCs at the start of the records. Processing is more complex since it may contain conditional processing to alter print characteristics based on conditions in the print file.

- Line mode with Overlays

  This type of file contains 3211 line data, and may contain carriage control bytes at the start of the records and/or TRCs at the start of the records. It also contains references to Overlays, which are merged with the Line Data.

- AFP Text only application

  This type of file is formatted entirely with AFP structured fields but does not contain references to Overlays or Graphics.

- AFP with Overlays and/or Page Segments

  This type of file is formatted entirely with AFP structured fields, but does contain references to Overlays or Page Segments, or contains them as inline objects.

- AFP with Overlays, Page Segments, and IOCA Images

  This type of file is formatted entirely with AFP structured fields, but also contains references to

Overlays or Page Segments containing IOCA image objects. What IOCA Function Set is in use.

- AFP with GOCA

  This type of file is formatted entirely with AFP structured fields, but contains references to GOCA objects, which are vector graphics usually generated by GDDM or a program invoking GDDM.

- AFP produced by ACIF including indexing structures

  This type of file is formatted entirely with AFP structured fields but does not contain references to Overlays or Graphics.

- AFP with Multi-Copy Statements

- Files with Custom Fonts

  These may have been purchased from IBM, a third party vendor, or created in-house with a tool like FLSF or one of the PC-based products. Remember that fonts may have been edited. Are there special characters in use?

- Unbounded Box Fonts

  These are the old 3800 style, usually starting with X1 through XG as coded font names.

- GraphMod Fonts

  These are some of the oldest fonts and often contain logos and signatures that date back to the earliest AFP installations.

- Color

  Do these documents contain highlight color or full color AFP?

- Shading

  Do these documents contain shading? If so, how was it put into the document? OGL? A font? A PSEG?

In a Xerox Environment...

What's the nature of the Xerox Print environment?

- Online, Offline or both?

  This is a critical question since the nature of the print files changes depending on the environment. If you operate in both modes, which jobs are printed in which mode?

- Line mode with basic DJDEs

  This is generally 3211 line data produced be an application, and conditioned with application-inserted DJDEs to change fonts, add FRMs and IMGs, and control output stacking.

- Line mode with complex DJDEs, including When=Change processing.

  This is the same as above except that it uses conditions in the line data to decide when to suppress or add text to the print.

- Line mode with FRMs

  Usually 3211 data with DJDEs calling form overlays.

- Line mode with LGOs.

  Usually 3211 line data with DJDEs calling .LGO files, which contain graphics or signatures.

- Line mode with graphics in FNT files

  Same as above except that the signature or graphic is stored as a font and requires that the data contain both the font call and the specification of the characters to produce the graphic.

- Line mode with IMGs

  Usually 3211 line data with DJDEs calling raster graphics stored as .IMG files. Printers generally require special graphics options and additional memory to support these types of graphics.

- Metacode with line/DJDE mix

  Mixed mode data can be complex Metacode interleaved with line data. These files normally print more slowly because the printer switches between line and Metacode mode.

- Metacode: text only application.

- Metacode with FRMs and/or IMGs

  Metacode interleaved with DJDEs to call the resources.

- Metacode with FRMs, Graphics in FNTS or LGOs

- Metacode with inline fonts

- DJDEs containing CMEs

- Custom or Encrypted Fonts

  These may have been purchased from Xerox or a third party

- Color: Highlight color

XES/UDK Printing: Decentralized Print

- Line/XES: Line mode with basic XES codes

- Line/XES: Line mode with complex XES codes, including Forms Merge

- Line/XES: Line mode with inline fonts

- Custom Fonts

- Inline Fonts

- What Escape character(s)are used

- Application-generated or coded by hand?

If you have PCL Printers...

- Line mode with basic codes

- Line mode with complex codes, including Forms Merge

- Line mode with downloadable soft fonts

- Custom Fonts

- Print driver generated or coded by hand

- Forms or fonts on cartridge

Add all of these considerations to your overall inventory and you should be able to discover all of the features of your corporate legacy data environment. But, don't forget that the inventory is not the end of the line. Even after you accomplish your migration, the world around you will keep on changing. Every time a vendor upgrades your software or hardware you may face new challenges.

Notice that we haven't mentioned those Jumbotrons or billboards? Here we go.

The same technologies that set you up to push data to cell phones and pagers may also let you push data to the large electronic billboards that you see in large malls and may also let you work with devices that use a new technology called electronic ink. IBM, Xerox and other companies have been working on the idea of electronic ink that paints an image on a special type of paper based on input from a computing device. Some companies have already piloted projects that drive data to large electronic ink billboards using cellular and pager technology. When these applications pay out their research costs and move into the general marketplace, you'll be ready for them!

Trailblazers

No one wants to be the first to work with legacy data, and we can assure you that *you* will not be the first. Over the past ten years, we have worked with a number of companies to help them migrate and share their corporate legacy data, and everyone ended in a success.

To give you an idea about those trailblazers, here is a quick look at some of those who have gone ahead.

A brokerage firm using AFP to print was facing a customer service issue. To provide a customer a copy of a current or past statement it was necessary to cause a batch transaction to generate the print, and then courier the hardcopy to the remote offices. Not only was it costly, but the lag in delivery was a customer service problem, especially at tax time. The solution was to insert a transform from AFP to PDF into their production environment, and then to build a web-enabled interface to locate the PDF version of the customer file in a disk archive when needed. From the PDF file the customer service people print the file or email it as needed.

That turned out to just be the beginning, though. Once they knew they could store and retrieve the PDF files, they expanded their project to provide access to their customers through a secure server. They faced some font matching issues and document segmentation issues in the early days of the project, but as a trailblazer they were one of the first to offer web access to customer statements.

Another early adopter was a bank that wanted to archive customer statement data and check images in PDF, but needed ability to reprint at high speed from the archive. PDF came to the rescue again, though this application had a few more hurdles to get over. In their PC environment they did not have a consistent font set on all machines, and that caused unreliable print in the early days of the project. With a bit of resource management and an effort to standardize the corporate desktop platform, though, they were very successful. They came back around and decided that their applications justified one more piece of technology, so they acquired a transform to print PDF to their AFP printers, too.

Finally, a print and mail bureau printing Xerox documents wanted to offer CD ROM delivery of customer data, segregated by broker/dealer or customer. The large print files were generated in Metacode, and not in any type of usable order. The solution was to add a Metacode to PDF transform to the environment, but with a twist. An addition piece of programming was added that cut the PDF file at the end of every account record and put it into a discrete directory on the server. At the end of the print run the CD was burned from the print server, with all of the account files in the appropriate directories. CDs could be cut for individual broker-dealers with only the accounts relevant to their customer base. While there were custom fonts in the Xerox datastream and not all of the resources were well-formed, each glitch was overcome and project was a success.

In Conclusion

Legacy data and emerging data types pose a huge challenge to anyone who works in information delivery. By this point you should have the tools you need to successfully embark on any project that involves taking legacy data and re-purposing it for the web, another printer, or even a cell phone screen.

We know that some of the technical folks will think we dusted too lightly over the topics, and some of the less technical folks may be overwhelmed. Our goal was to walk that fine line between the two worlds, and we'll welcome hearing from you if there are things you think we can improve.

Good luck, and let us know how it works for you. You can reach us at info@mcgrewmcdaniel.com.

Appendix A:
Where to Find Help

In Appendix C, we will look at the vendors who work in this space, but here we want to concentrate on all of the other types of help you can find through user groups, industry conferences, and list serves. Over time, this list will expand and contract, so if you discover that a resource has disappeared, please let us know by sending a note to info@mcgrewmcdaniel.com.

List Serves

The two that we rely on are the AFP-L and Xerox-L, both initiated by the XPLOR Electronic Document Association. Both are Topica Lists that you can subscribe to at www.topica.com. At this moment, the Xerox list is moderated by industry expert Bill Dossett, while the AFP List is in the very capable hands of Michael Botos, EDP. There is a world of helpful people, and these lists seem to be on the radar of most of the experts willing to lend a hand. The marketing is kept to a minimum, but you will find vendors answering generic questions and asking questions, too.

We would be remiss if we did not mention the Document Strategy list hosted by Kevin Craine, EDP. Here is where you will find lively exchanges of information on how to sell a document strategy in your organization. This is a Yahoo list. To send messages to this group, send an email to documentstrategy@yahoogroups.com. Messages are delivered via e-mail to all members. You

can view and send messages through the web by
going to http://groups.yahoo.com/group/documentstrategy/
messages.

Ezines and Newsletters

It is almost impossible to keep up with the explosion of
helpful resources on the Internet. Here are some that we
use frequently, but remember that it's only a subset of all of
the possibilities.

DevWebPro: DevWebPro.com is a place to start for any
question about web-based application development. Their
newsletter offers practical solutions and code you can
borrow!

Enterprise Systems Journal: www.esj.com is a great source
of information that applies specifically to the enterprise,
covering the mainframe and network environments and the
applications that support them.

eStats and eMarketer: www.emarketer.com is the source for
a number of daily and weekly newsletters that can keep
you up to date on trends in the ecommerce world. The
newsletters are free, but they do run a fee-based research
service.

Fast Company: www.fastcompany.com covers the rapidly
changing corporate landscape, offering articles on
everything from human resource development to
implementing technology.

FreePint: www.FreePint.com is a UK-based community that
excels at finding obscure facts. They have a list serve for
posting and answering questions, a job listing service, a
book review section, and pointers to thousands of valuable
resources. There is a free component and a subscription
component.

InformationWeek: www.informationweek.com is a great general purpose source for information on everything to do with technology in information delivery applications.

InternetWeek: www.internetweek.com covers the Internet from top to bottom. There is some cross over with the wireless and mobile computing ezines, but we still take all of them.

JOHO: www.hyperorg.com is the Journal of the Hyperlinked Organization, hosted by Dr. David Weinberger. This is a great forum for picking up what's really hot and what's really old news.

Killen Report: www.killen.com appears on each Monday with business intelligence concerning companies in the EBPP and EIPP space.

iSource: isource.ibm.com gives you all of that information that used to be available only from your corporate IBM site representative. Now, you sign up, specify what products you are interested in, and they do the rest. If you work in Europe, there are even country-specific versions available. This is currently a free service.

Mbusiness: www.MbusinessDaily.com is a great source of breaking news concerning mobile applications.

MC2: www.mcgrewmcdaniel.com hosts a monthly newsletter covering emerging technology, information delivery, and news you can use.

MIT Technology Review: www.technologyreview.com covers what's in the labs.

PDFZone: www.pdfzone.com is the first stop we make when we are looking for information on PDF plug-ins, transforms, and product enhancements. Their newsletter always has the latest vendor news and information about the latest applications for PDF and the emerging world of PDF-based interchange and document management standards. This is currently a free service.

PrintPlanet: www.printplant.com (formerly WhatTheyThink) has a free and subscription component. This is a great source for people who work across the boundaries of MIS Print and digital and offset printing outside of IT.

PrintWriter: www.printwriter.com has a wide array of resources, news from the industry, and expert advice columns.

TDAN: The Data Administration Newsletter www.tdan.com

User Interface Engineering: www.uie.com is one of the best sources for information on web design and document design for the web.

Wireless Week: www.wirelessweek.com provides a daily newsletter on breaking news in wireless applications.

User Groups and Associations

AIIM (Association for Information and Image Management): www.aiim.org

American Forest and Paper Association: www.afandpa.org

Association of Graphic Communications (AGC): www.agcomm.org

Assoc. of Suppliers of Printing and Publishing: www.npes.org

BFMA (Business Forms Management Association): www.bfma.org

DAMA: The Data Management Association: www.dama.org

Digital Printing and Imaging Association: www.dpia.org

Document Management Industry Association: www.dmia.org

Graphic Communications Association: www.gca.org

IBM Computer Users' Association (UK): www.ibm-cua.org.uk

International Prepress Association: www.ipa.org

International Publishing Management Association: www.ipmass.org

National Association of Printers and Lithographers (NAPL): www.napl.org

National Paper Trade Association: www.gonpta.com

Paper Industry Management Association: www.pima-online.com

PC Association (UK): www.pcassoc.org

Printing Industries of America (PIA): www.printing.org

PIRA: www.piranet.com

PrintImage International: www.printimage.org

Printing Industries of America: www.gain.net

SHARE: www.share.org

The Association for Work Process Improvement: www.tawpi.org

The Websphere User Group: www.websphere.org

Xplor International: www.xplor.org

Standards Bodies

The following is a list of some of the standards bodies that might be useful. They are not all of the standards organizations or consortiums since that list grows weekly.

American National Standards Institute (ANSI): web.ansi.org. maintains information for standards developers, including a comprehensive list of resources at http://web.ansi.org/public/library/internet/resources.html.

International Electrotechnical Commission (IEC): www.iec.ch IEC was founded in 1906 to promote international co-operation on all questions of standardization and related matters in the fields of electrical and electronic engineering.

Internet Engineering Task Force (IETF): www.ietf.cnri.reston.va.us. IETF is a community of network designers, operators, vendors, and researchers working to ensure the smooth evolution of the Internet architecture and operation of the Internet.

Internet Architecture Board (IAB): www.iab.org/iab/. IAB provides oversight of the process used to create Internet Standards.

Internet Society (ISOC): www.isoc.org. ISOC is the home for the groups responsible for Internet infrastructure standards, including the IETF and IAB.

International Organisation for Standardisation (ISO): www.iso.ch. ISO is a worldwide federation of national standards bodies from 130 countries, promoting standards in all fields, including information technology. SGML was codified as an ISO standard, laying the groundwork for HTML and XML.

National Automated Clearinghouse Association (NACHA): www.nacha.org. NACHA develops operating rules and business practices for the Automated Clearing House (ACH) Network and for other areas of electronic payments.

The Unicode Consortium: www.unicode.org. The Unicode Consortium brings together software industry corporations and researchers at the leading edge of standardizing international character encoding.

World Wide Web Consortium (W3C): www.w3c.org.

And don't forget to check the conferences and user group meetings!

Appendix B:
Vendor Manuals

Adobe PostScript Language Manuals

Reference manuals authored by Adobe on the PostScript
language include the following:

PostScript Language Reference, third edition (Red Book)
ISBN 0-201-37922-8

PostScript Language Tutorial and Cookbook (Blue Book)
ISBN 0-201-10179-3

PostScript Language Program Design (Green Book) ISBN
0-201-14396-8

Adobe Type 1 Font Format (Black Book) ISBN 0-201-
57044-0

Programming the Display PostScript with X (Orange
Book) ISBN 0-201-62203-3

Programming Display PostScript with NEXTSTEP
(Purple Book) ISBN 0-201-58135-3

HP Manuals

HP LaserJet 5P and 5MP Printer User's Manual (English):
C3150-99025

HP PCL/PJL Technical Reference Package: Includes HP
PCL 5 Printer Language Technical Reference Manual,
Printer Job Language Technical Reference Manual,

HP PCL/PJL Technical Quick Reference Guide, and the HP PCL Comparison Guide: 5021-0377

HP PCL/PJL Technical Reference CD Bundle: Includes HP PCL 5 Printer Language Technical Reference Manual, Printer Job Language Technical Reference Manual, HP PCL/PJL Technical Quick Reference Guide, and the HP PCL Comparison Guide: C5961-0976

HP LaserJet 5MP Printer Macintosh Notes (English): C3155-90901

HP LaserJet 5P/5MP Quick Reference Card (English): C3980-91078

HP LaserJet 5P/5MP Printer Service Manual (English Only): C3980-91078

The technical reference manual contains a complete description of PCL 5. The developer's guide contains many software examples illustrating how to design PCL-compatible software.

IBM Manuals Related to Printing

Font Object Content Architecture Reference (June 2000) S544-3285-04

Intelligent Printer Data Stream Reference (March 1996) S544-3417-05

Bar Code Object Content Architecture Reference (June 2000) S544-3766-03

Advanced Function Presentation: Programming Guide and Line Data Reference (October 2000) S544-3884-02

IBM Dictionary of Printing (March 1995) G544-3973-00

Data Stream and Object Architectures: Graphics Object Content Architecture for Advanced Function Presentation Reference (October 2000) S544-5498-01

Data Stream and Object Architectures: Mixed Object
Document Content Architecture Reference (April
2001) SC31-6802-05

Data Stream and Object Architectures: Presentation Text
Object Content Architecture Reference (August 1997)
SC31-6803-02

IBM Redbooks Related to Printing

AFP Printing in an IBM Cross-System Environment,
GG24-3765-00 Red*book*, published August-24-1994

IBM AS/400 Printing V, SG24-2160-01 Red*book*, published
October-24-2000

Distributing AFP Printing from a Host System, GG24-
4493-00 Red*book*, published November-29-1994

Printing for Fun and Profit Under AIX V4, GG24-3570-01
Red*book*, published December-13-1994

IBM AS/400 Printing IV, GG24-4389-00 Red*book*,
published January-30-1995

IBM AS/400 Printing III, GG24-4028-00 Red*book*,
published June-30-1993

AFP Printing for SAP Using R/3 and R/2, SG24-4629-00
Red*book*, published November-29-1995

Printing for Fun and Profit under AIX 5L, SG24-6018-00
Red*book*, published March-7-2001

Printing with MVS on the IBM PC Server System/390,
SG24-4612-00 Red*book*, published January-13-1996

IBM Network Station Printing Guide, SG24-5212-00
Red*book*, published May-27-1998

Font Specification Manuals

Adobe Technical Note #5176: "The Compact Font Format Specification."

Adobe Technical Note #5177: "Type 2 Charstring Format."

TrueType 1.0 Font Files, Technical Specification. Microsoft.

OpenType Layout Font Specification. Microsoft.

Adobe Type 1 Font Format: Addison Wesley, 1991; ISBN 0-201-57044-0.

Adobe Technical Note #5015: "The Type 1 Font Format Supplement.": This document contains all updates to the Type 1 format.

Adobe Technical Note #5088 "Font Naming Issues.": This document discusses general font name issues.

Appendix C:
Vendors and Their Offerings

The legacy data market space is a mature one with many vendors and consultants who stand ready to help you work through any type of legacy data project you might have. This appendix is not intended to be a comprehensive list. There are hundreds of companies around the world who work with legacy data, with new companies emerging and existing companies merging every day. What follows, though, will get you started on the road to finding the best solutions for your needs. Talk to as many vendors as you can find, and give them as much information as you can so that they can make the best suggestions for your situation.

The product descriptions below were provided by the vendors or acquired from their marketing material. Contact the vendor with any questions. Contact us at info@mcgrewmcdaniel.com if you find any inaccuracies or have an addition.

Adobe: www.adobe.com

Adobe® Acrobat® 5.0 software lets you convert any document to an Adobe Portable Document Format (PDF) file. Anyone can open your document across a broad range of hardware and software, and it will look exactly as you intended — with layout, fonts, links, and images intact. With Acrobat 5.0, you and your team can increase productivity by approving and commenting on documents from within a Web browser.

AFPSoft: www.afpsoft.de

AFP FONT CONVERTER: AFP Font Converter converts an AFP font into Adobe's Type1 or/and Microsoft's TrueType Format.

AFP RESOURCE DISPATCHER: AFP Resource Dispatcher determines which resources are needed, whether they exist in your current print environment and if they have the correct resolution.

PAGE DEF EXPLORER: The PageDef Explorer tool is a program to display binary AFP PageDef resources and convert into PPFA text. The PageDef Explorer lets you view, print and search an AFP page definition in a convenient readable form. You can transform PageDefs into PPFA for further processing.

FORM DEF EXPLORER: The FormDef Explorer tool is a program to display binary AFP FormDef resources and convert into PPFA text. The FormDef Explorer lets you view, print and search an AFP form definition in a convenient readable form. You can transform FormDefs into PPFA for further processing.

PAGE DEF CONVERTER: The PageDef Converter tool is a program to transform 240 dpi PageDef resources into 300 dpi PageDefs. Supports multi-file conversion.

FORM DEF CONVERTER: The FormDef Converter tool is a program to transform 240 dpi FormDef resources into 300 dpi FormDefs. Supports multi-file conversion.

MIGRATE: Currently MIGRATE can convert CAT's (Character Arrangement Tables) into AFP code pages and MXM's (Matrix Modules) into AFP font character sets with 240 dpi. Also creates coded fonts, i.e. pairs of code page and font character set names.

American Printware, Inc: www.apwi.com

PalServe, DJDEServe (Formerly PXLServe), 4235Serve, IPDSServe, DocWeaver, DocCluster, DocBuilder, DocSpooler, and SocketPrinting are products specifically designed to assist in distributing mainframe generated Xerox and IBM-based printing information across an enterprise-wide distributed data processing network where shared resources require specific data conversion technologies and additional printing functionality. These software products are designed to convert, control, manage and monitor printing requirements and output throughout a network scheme that utilizes mixed CPU protocols, equipment and resources.

Anacomp: www.anacomp.com

Using ANACOMP's Data Transmission Services (DTS), print streams or images are transferred to an Anacomp Web Presentment service center where they are received, logged, and processed for viewing. Once processed, they are instantly accessible by any authorized user from the Internet or your private intranet. While the documents are available for viewing for many years, ANACOMP also provides alternate near-line and archival media for when your access requirements diminish.

ASE Technologies, Inc.: www.ase-tech.com

ASE Data Distributor takes output from your existing applications and distributes it for printing, viewing, e-mailing, faxing, the web and/or conversion.

Barr Systems: www.barrsystems.com

Barr Enterprise Print Server: The complete print and document management solution

BARR/PRINT to Metacode: Print from Windows applications to channel-attached Xerox printers.

Barr Enterprise Communications Server: The versatile, custom-built enterprise networking solution .

SNA Gateway Connection Products: Featuring products for high-speed connectivity between mainframes and SNA gateways via the S/390 ESCON® or Bus & Tag Channels or via SDLC.

SDK: Featuring Software Development Kits (SDK) for S/390 Channel connectivity.

DOS-based Printing and File Transfer Products: Featuring our legendary products for remote printing and file transfer including BARR/RJE, PRINT370, PRINT/CHANNEL, and more.

BMC Software: www.bmc.com

CONTROL-D for OS/390 and CONTROL-D for Distributed Systems. The CONTROL-D product line has been on the market for over 10. CONTROL-D provides a full range of report and document management functions including data capture and analysis, storage and archiving, distribution and end-user access. It supports a variety of datastreams including IBM AFP, Xerox LCDS, and Xerox Metacode as well as conventional ASA and machine carriage control data.

Cincom: www.cincom.com

iD Web Document Services: Generate personalized
communications using the World Wide Web.

iD Text™ and iD Workstation™ : Manage large volumes
of complex documents, professionally and quickly.

iD Report™ : Improve revenues with high speed,
intelligent production of statements, invoices, and
forms.

iD CinDoc™ : Improve your document archives with a
database that sorts, indexes, and stores information
linked to documents for easy retrieval.

Comparex: www.comparex.de

COMPAREX Migration Architecture, COMPAREX Migration
Center, COMPAREX Migration Methodology - will help
organizations to take immediate advantage of the business
and economic opportunities of open systems without
the risk, expense, or delay of complete application
re-engineering.

Crawford Technologies: www.crawfordtech.com

Pro/Meta PDF outputs PDF documents that can be used
for e-statement applications in EBPP systems, bill
presentment and report distributions.

Pro/Meta AFP Converts Xerox documents to Advanced
Function Printing AFPDS format for use with
InfoPrint Manager and other AFP products.

Pro/Meta PCL creates PCL output for distributed printing
and print proofing purposes.

Pro/Meta API allows software developers to utilize Xerox
Metacode, LCDS, DJDE, FNT, IMG, FRM, and JSL

objects in applications such as EBPP, COLD, RDMS systems and Print Servers.

Pro/Meta Normalization and Indexing Facility (PMNIF) allows large print files to be split into individual statements and indexed for later retrieval.

Pro/Meta PostScript Extraction extracts data from PostScript files and splits PostScript files into subdocuments.

Pro/Meta PCL to AFP converts form PCL to Advanced Function Printing AFPDS.

Pro/Meta AFP to PDF converts from Advanced Function Printing AFPDS to Adobe PDF format.

Creative Document Automation:
www.afp-software.com

AFP Lookup:

- Windows-Look and familiar explorer style
- Analysis of all AFP files (AFP, Page Segments, Overlays, Fonts, etc.)
- Presentation of all AFP objects (Presentation Text, GOCA, IOCA, Bar Code, etc.)
- Supplementation of all Structured Fields and Triplets
- Supplementation of all NOP records and indices
- No code page problems through 70 included code pages
- Analysis of AFP files with many megabyte in size
- Analysis of many AFP files at the same time
- Multi-language support (currently English and German)
- Search-function in the analyzed file

CSP Aktiengesellschaft: www.csp.de

Mercury: Mercury collects the print data from different origins such as mainframe computers and PC networks. The data is distributed to wherever it is required - to printers, fax machines, copiers, PDF (new!), internet, or other components.

Because the printers of different manufacturers do only understand certain languages (data streams), the incoming data has to be translated (converted). Mercury does that conversion.

Attachments

      Parallel IN / OUT
      Ethernet IN / OUT
      Fast Ethernet IN / OUT
      Token Ring IN / OUT
      ESCON IN
      Channel IN / OUT (Bus & Tag)
      SCSI OUT

Emulations

      DJDE / Meta to PCL/PDF
      XES to PCL/PDF
      IPDS to PCL/PDF
      IGP to PCL/PDF
      IPDS to DJDE / Meta
      PCL to DJDE / Meta / PDF
      EBCDIC to ASCII
      PCL Pass Through
      PostScript Pass Through UDE

Danka: www.danka.com

Danka offers solutions for business applications, and consults on integrated business solutions.

DocuCorp, Inc: www.docucorp.com

DocuCreate products create forms that can be used over and over in high-volume environments. It includes editors that create forms and insert fields for run-time variable data insertion. It produces device-independent data streams that can be printed, archived and distributed over intranets and the Internet.

DocuSave is a full-scale archival system that automates the storage and indexing of documents and enables clients to retrieve, view, annotate and route them as needed.

DocuMaker performs data merging, document assembly and business rules creation to automate enterprise wide document production for such applications as insurance policies and bill statement presentment. It provides device-independent technologies that enable individualized printing, archiving and delivery via networks and the Web.

Document Sciences, Inc.: www.documentsciences.com

CompuSet: CompuSet assembles and formats documents and prepares a CompuSet Intermediate File (CIF) for output processing to Web or print, using one of Document Sciences' Emitters.

Print Emitters transform a composed document to Page Description Languages (PDLs). PDL formats currently supported include:

- Xerox Metacode
- Adobe PostScript
- IBM AFP
- HP PCL5
- Adobe PDF
- CreoScitex Variable Print Specification (VPS)

Elixir Technologies : www.elixir.com

Elixir's Transformation Suite converts legacy print streams to your choice of PostScript, PCL, PDF, and TIFF. AFP and XML are scheduled for 4Q01. The input formats that are supported are Xerox Line Data (DJDE), 3211 Line Data, Xerox Metacode, AFP, and PCL. PDF and XML input are scheduled.

PageMiner provides a solution for extracting data from legacy print streams such as Xerox DJDE Line Data, Metacode or AFP. Extracted from the print file, this data is available for use in eCommerce applications, can be passed to a document composition system like Elixir's Opus product, or build an external index for archival systems.

When converting a legacy print file to PDF, the extracted data can be used to build an external index, bookmark the PDF, or split the file into individual PDFs.

Elixir's Desktop and Converter products for Xerox or IBM will provide font conversions as well as form and graphic conversions.

Emtex Limited: www.emtex.com

Emtex VIP : Production Print Server offering PDL transforms and automatic resource conversions, queue/printer management.

- Input: AFP, LCDS(DJDE & Metacode), PS, PDF (via channel, lpr/lpd, watched folders, SCSI-tape, MVS-JES2, VSE/Power)
- Outputs: IPDS, LCDS (Metacode), AFPDS, PCL, PS, PDF, TIFF, Viewer (Color & monochrome)
- Additional functions: Indexing, Reprint, Viewing, Central Resource Management (Xerox LPS printers)
- Automatic reprint (from Inserters or integrity systems), DocEnhance for electronic inserts, document modification, currency conversions (runs on Windows NT, Windows 2000, & OS/2)

A subset of VIP is offered as a Development Station for application development and proofing (VIP does not do document composition). VIP is OEM'd by Océ as Prisma X+ (formerly PS8000).

Exstream Software : www.exstream.com

Dialogue combines personalized document creation, campaign management, tracking and content management in one tool.

Printer resources creation & resource management: All design is done with outline fonts (Adobe Type 1, TrueType or OpenType) and an integrated desktop tool or an ActiveX control integrated into Quark, In-Design, Illustrator, Corel, Word, PowerPoint, Excel and others. Dialogue generates the appropriate resources based on the design by creating floating virtual overlays and integrating them into the print output as appropriate. Dialogue builds all needed fonts from the outline fonts, converting to AFP Xerox and PCL as needed, including kerning pairs, codepages, and metrics. Dialogue can hide all of the resource management or generate all of the resources so that they can be loaded to the printer/resource library.

Print mining: Dialogue can mine all the data from a print stream, then create any type of re-designed output to change the complete look of a document. Delivery can be to the web (XML, HTML via XSLT, PDF, RTF), or to PDLs.

Other source of legacy data: Dialog reads multiple input files simultaneously, in any format (delimited, record based, database). Dialogue can analyze a standard COBOL copybook and build all the linkage to read any type of COBOL.

Group 1 Software: www.g1.com

DOC1: DOC1 has two primary components, a design workstation running Windows NT and a multi-platform production engine. Document applications can be created on a PC, then hosted in any environment: mainframe, client/server, or PC. Users develop the application on the PC using intuitive drag-and-drop techniques similar to those found in desktop publishing packages. DOC1 gives full control over typography, alignment, and graphics.

Message1: Marketers can create and manage highly targeted, revenue-driving messaging campaigns with minimal IT involvement.

DOC1 for Workgroups: Version control and content management facilitate collaborative development and accelerate moving applications into production.

IBM: www.printers.ibm.com

Infoprint Designer for iSeries:
- Provides a fully graphical document design system for the iSeries
- Facilitates access to the printing capabilities of the iSeries, featuring AFP and IPDS
- Enables easy development of iSeries native print resources
- Integrates completely with iSeries servers: from design through printing and "e-output"
- Designed for the non-programmer, providing ease of use, functionality and precision
- Delivers an affordable, comprehensive e-business solution AFP Printsuite and Utilities for iSeries
- Print to network IPDS printers with standard iSeries reliability and control

IBM Advanced Print Utility for iSeries
- Enables conversion of simple output applications to electronic documents through an interactive user

interface

- Requires no programming changes are made to the application because it is application independent
- Supports bar codes, outline fonts, images and electronic forms
- Allows multiple copies of application data to be printed with individually tailored content and design

And also:

- IBM Page Printer Formatting Aid (iSeries)
- Page Printer Formatting Aid for Windows NT and Windows 2000
- Page Printer Formatting Aid/370
- Document Composition Facility/370
- Overlay Generation Language/370
- IBM AFP Font Collection
- AFP Toolbox
- AFP Workbench
- Infoprint Server
- AFP Utilities for iSeries
- Print Services Facility

Also, look at IBM DeveloperWorks at http://www-106.ibm.com/developerworks/ for the latest information on what IBM has in the lab. For more information on integrating you host legacy environment with the web, take a look at IBM's WebSphere Developer page at http://www7b.boulder.ibm.com/wsdd/.

AFP Font Collection

Type Families —Core Interchange: Times New Roman, Helvetica, Courier, APL, OCR A & B, Prestige, Letter Gothic, Gothic Text, Boldface, Gothic Katakana

Typeface Styles —Roman Medium, Roman Bold, Italic Medium, Italic Bold

Font Technologies and Resolutions —240-pel bitmaps, 300-pel bitmaps, AFP outlines, Adobe® Type 1 outlines, Double-Byte Character Set (DBCS) outlines for Simplified and Traditional Chinese, Japanese and Korean

Language Complements —Supports 48 languages; other languages available outside of Core Interchange Set, including Euro currency symbol support

Type Transformer and Utilities for Windows —Type 1 and CID-keyed outline fonts

I-data – see MPI Tech

IKON Office Solutions: www.ikon.com

IKON's digital document technologies and electronic repositories provide search- and print-on-demand capabilities that save both time and space.

ISIS - Papyrus: www/isis-papyrus.com

- WYSIWYG PC workstation based dynamic business document design for batch and client/server
- Data consolidation and management without changes to your existing applications
- Production formatting on the platform of your choice from MVS to UNIX to any Intel OS
- Campaign management for a multi-channel, electronic and print marketing approach
- Post production, sorting, postal sequencing, discounting, enveloping and inserter controls
- Client/Server interactive document generation with total compatibility to mass production
- Business document distribution and workflow management
- Network print management and print servers for IPDS, Xerox, PCL5 and Postscript, and Scitex
- Internet document distribution and presentation in HTML/GIF, Java, AFP and PDF
- Short-term re-print staging and long-term archiving

L&K: www.l-en-k.nl or www.dokumentdialog.de

L&K is a distributor of many document tools and a consultancy. They are currently distributors of these products:

- DOC1
- Visual PCE
- Xenos d2e
- Elixir Opus
- Elixir
- VIP
- StreamWeaver
- RSD-EOS
- RSD Folders
- Fonts

LCI Intermate: www.intermate-us.com

LCI Intermate supplies LAN and IBM printer connectivity and network security solutions, including hardware and software printer connectivity solutions to VPN and secure printing solutions. Intermate solutions represent the following categories: Coax/Twinax Connectivity, LAN Connectivity, Host Software Connectivity, Electronic Forms, New Technology and Technical Services.

Lytrod Software: www.lytrod.com

Proform Designer is geared towards supporting multiple, or migrating between, production print environments. This includes Xerox's LPS and NPS line, PCL and AFP. It's bit-by-bit form and resource conversion creates identical output regardless of the platform. Convert an entire application to a new platform by simply loading and saving the form. The Windows 95, WYSIWYG design environment is instantly familiar and simple to navigate. Customizable toolbars provide quick access to all of Proform Designer's drawing, formatting, and text editing tools. Easily access TrueType

fonts and import graphics (PCX, TIFF, GIF, JPEG, BMP).
Supports:

- Xerox LPS production printers
- Xerox NPS production printers
- AFP printers
- Other PostScript & PCL printers
- VIPP

BitCopy - Font editing and conversion utility

ImageCopy - Image editing and conversion utility

Maas: www.maas.de or www.afp2web.de

AFP2WEB: Converts AFP or TIFF files to PDF, JPEG,
ASCII or TIFF in Windows NT or UNIX environments.

XML4COBOL: A Java-based Graphical DTD editor and a
parser/mapper provide a fast path to XML solutions
for mainframe environments.

Metavante (formerly M & I Data Systems):
www.metavante.com

CSF Document Composition: CSF helps create,
revise and manage customer communications such
as statements, bills, letters, and notices. CSF is
the software solution for personalized customer
communications, delivering new customer
communication concepts in a fraction of the time
of alternatives. CSF uses standard word processing
functionality, which enables customers to visually
display each document as it is built and tested,
as well as implement true one-to-one customer
marketing via customized customer documents.

MPI Tech (incorporating I-data): www.i-data.com

EPM™: Enterprise Print Manager - One integrated system manages all OS/390 printing processes

PSS: AFP printer driver for PCL, PostScript and PDF devices on MVS, OS/390 and VM.

NearStar: www.nearstar.com

Dynamic DataServer: A Job Manager that can run on Windows NT & 2000, various UNIX platforms. Integrated into DDS is a Xerox LCDS & Metacode to PDF & PCL transform. It has the ability to pre-process data prior to routing to the destination.

ObjectifLune: www.objectiflune.com

PlanetPress: A printer centric electronic forms solution that enables laser printers to be used in variable data printing applications with data from almost any host. PlanetPress forms, running on the printer controller, enable complex, high-speed variable data printing applications to be developed with ease in a Windows point and click design interface. When used in conjunction with PlanetPress Watch enables output management including distributed printing and electronic document delivery.

Océ: www.oce.com

Océ PRISMA: One solution for many environments.

Océ PRISMAproduction: Print server (PC or mainframe) for centralized and decentralized production printing.

Océ PRISMAaudit ®: Professional document management system that tracks and controls the digital workflow.

Option Software: www.optionsoft.com

Advanced Printing System Interface (APSI): The ultimate front-end for Xerox centralized printing systems with job setup automation, multimedia, stock database, detailed trail log and activity reporting. Built-in security and remote control provide and open interface to your printing systems without any configuration changes.

Enterprise Server: Option Enterprise Server extends the functionality of the Site Server by interconnecting multiple sites. Virtually all functions of the Site Server can be performed from the enterprise server.

InfoAccess (IA): Detailed accurate page accounting for charge-back billing and production monitoring.

Librarian (L): Xerox resource management and tracking with version control and multiple developer support.

Process Control Center (PCC): Option PCC is a shop floor job tracking system with a network of one or more data entry and monitoring stations throughout the production area. A complete PCC system includes Master Station, General Stations, Dedicated Stations and the Automated Stations.

PROM Server Plus (PSP): PSP is a network-oriented control and management system for multiple Xerox LPS, NPS and IPDS devices in any printing center. PSP includes the PROM Management Console which functions as a master station to setup, control and monitor multiple printing systems, which have been equipped with the Option Advanced Printing System Interface (APSI) feature.

PICT Systems: www.pictsystems.com

PICT Systems covers a broad range of areas such as IBM AFP and Xerox printing, distributed printing, documents on demand, document design and composition, report and document management solutions, through to every possible variation of systems architecture, implementation and integration.

Pitney Bowes: www.pitneybowes.com

docSense Professionals help customers set a strategic course, one based on their unique business situation. For businesses whose success depends on the mission critical use of leading edge systems and technology, docSense maps customized solutions that make the most of investments in technology and people. Innovative approaches to customer problems - at rates 50 percent to 80 percent faster than most in-house solutions - docSense Professional Services partners with leading tech businesses to help them improve and take control of processes.

Pitney Bowes Software Systems: www.pitneysoft.com

StreamWeaver: Support mixing of all major print streams, including PCL, line data, AFP, AFPDS, DJDE and Metacode, and PostScript® derived from multiple applications to create a single output printstream.

StreamWeaver is used to:

- Enable intelligent inserting by adding or changing finishing control barcodes such as OMR or Code 3of9
- Maximize the effectiveness of software used for address cleansing and presorting
- Consolidate into one envelope multiple documents intended for the same recipient
- Facilitate the migration from one-up simplex to multiple-up duplex printing
- Customize documents and mailings for highly personalized communications and 1:to:1 target marketing efforts

PrintSoft: www.printsoftamericas.com or
www.printsoft.com..au

PReS for Xerox, Scitex, IBM and Océ Printing Systems:
PReS, Printer Resource Software, is a PC- based software
package has the following features:

- Text and Data Merging
- Text Positioning
- Dynamic Graphics
- Wordwrap
- "Userhook" instruction
- Formatting Arguments
- Language Sensitive Formatting
- Numeric Arrays
- Print Control/Job Control
- Interleaved Graphics

TransForm: Convert PC graphics to graphics ready for high
speed electronic print systems. TransFont: Create fonts for
a range of high speed electronic printers from TrueType
and PostScript outlines. BarCode Toolkit:Now you can print
a wide range of barcodes on any printer supported by
PReS. PReS Archiving Solution: Now you can use the
familiar PReS scripting environment to archive and retrieve
documents.

Red Titan: www.redtitan.com

The RedTitan document design system optimises
information systems by integrating data into mass-
customised documents.

- Document design and composition for high volume
  database publishing.
- Supports all industry standard printers and e-formats.
- Runs on PC under Microsoft Windows.
- WYSIWYG interface with access to source language.
- Sophisticated 'conditional' data handling and viewing
  features.
- Multi-page composition.

The Red Titan Legacy Migration System:

- Emulates all the features of Xerox centralised printers on VIPP, PostScript, PCL and AFP printers.
- Runs on PC under Microsoft Windows.
- Migration path from Xerox DJDE to new systems.
- Lets you test and debug jobs with live data and view pages on screen.
- Allows production runs on an office printer if mainframe printer is down

The Red Titan Font Kit:

- Inputs and outputs to any printer format.
- Converts TrueType and PostScript fonts to bitmap format.
- Creates special font effects, accented characters, etc. Double byte font management option.
- Scanner interface with colour image editing.
- PCL Intellifont to Xerox MRP conversion.
- Cartridge programming.
- Professional file editing and management tools

Sefas Technologies: www.sefas.com

Open Print is a suite of software products that enable an Automated Document Factory from flat file or legacy PDL in to complete integrity of outgoing envelope content. The products are as follows:

Studio: Raw data to composed documents. Objects imported from Windows applications; Script or drag and drop. Includes colour; logos; data driven graphics and the following output Print Descriptor Languages: AFP; PCL; Metacode; IJPDS; PostScript; PDF; HTML; XML; Bitmap

Remake: Legacy PDL's (AFP, PCL and Metacode) transformed to all the Studio output PDL's and with the potential addition of all the features facilitated by Studio.

Delivery: The ability to split or merge printstreams allowing batching for economic production. Finishing marks imposed at the last stage. Postal sortation enabled. Selective reprinting of documents enabled.

Director: Job processing control and reprinting; job enquiries and management reporting; system control and housekeeping. Single screen control of print room operations.

Projector: Browser access to documents created by Studio and Remake with search ability and three levels of interaction. Currently Intranet only.

Solimar Systems: www.solimarsystems.com

Printer Connectivity and Centralized Queue Management: The Solimar Connectivity Server is a front-end solution for Xerox LPS printers. The server provides host to printer connectivity, centralized job and resource management and the ability to print network PCL and PostScript applications to LPS printers.

Print Director: The Solimar Print/Director System is a modular production print server that provides integrated host to printer connectivity, dynamic data stream (PDL) conversions, and sophisticated queue management. PDL support for:

- ASCII/EBCDIC
- Data Blocking
- IPDS
- PCL 4, 5c, 5e
- PDF
- PostScript 2, 3
- SCS
- TIFF
- Xerox DJDE LCDS/Metacode

SOLSearcher: SOLsearcher is a suite of plug-ins for Adobe Acrobat and Reader. The plug-ins provide a method for rapidly locating information within PDF documents. SOLindexer is used to graphically define index fields,

SOLmonitor automatically indexes PDF documents, and SOLfinder provides the interface end users use to search indexed documents.

TUKANDA is specialized document composition and printing software for Microsoft Windows that makes it easy to convert a database into a gold mine of personalized correspondence. The core of TUKANDA is an object-oriented composition engine that weds a user-friendly interface with powerful database integration and document formatting capabilities. Support the following output:

- AFPDS spool formats
- IPDS
- IJPDS
- PCL
- PDF
- PostScript
- Windows GDI

XIMAGE is a printer driver that creates Xerox form overlays, images, and Metacode print streams from virtually any Windows application and PDF file. This driver simplifies the task of making electronic document forms for environments with Xerox applications.

Spur Products Corporation: www.spur.com

SB/2K Deluxe is a complete hardware and software connectivity solution that connects and manages centralized printers in today's sophisticated network environments. The easily configured management capabilities include resource management, DJDE insertion, data conversion, and banner pages. Replaces products formerly called the SpurBox/2000+ and the PPCII.

SB/2K Express is a family of plug and play protocol converters which connect a single centralized printer to a single host or Ethernet network. The Express family consists of over 50 custom interfaces to connect today's high end and yesterday' s legacy midrange and mainframe computers. Replaces products formerly called USAII and System 534.

TallPine Corporation: www.tallpine.com

AFP PageMapper™ utility converts AFP to XML.

ResourceManager analyzes and manages resources required by your AFP files.

FontManager helps you analyze your font usage.

TallPine MSFLib™ to help index and store your AFP data.

TallPine DataMorf™ to create AFP from your PC/Workstation databases.

Xenos: www.xenos.com

The Xenos d2e Platform™ e-business infrastructure software transforms complex legacy data and documents into industry-standard e-content formats for presentment on the Web. Its component-based architecture allows for the selection of the specific technology needed to transform data from disparate sources into Web-ready formats, including XML, HTML, WML, and PDF.

Xerox Corporation: www.xerox.com

Xerox and Xerox Business Systems sell solutions in the legacy data space. They OEM the Emtex VIPP solution, and partner with a number of other vendors. See the Xerox website for details.

Glossary

Advanced Function Presentation Data Stream (AFPDS): The documented application data stream for AFP, including composed text pages, graphics and other resources.

AFP: Advanced Function Printing/Presentation. Includes all forms of files that print on IBM AFP printers through Print Services Facility (PSF).

All-Points-Addressability (APA): The ability to position text and images at any defined point on the printable area of the paper.

API: Application Program Interface. Sometimes also called a toolkit, or SDK (Software Development Kit).

ASCII / American Standard Code for Information Interchange: ASCII is the most common format for text files in computers and on the Internet. In an ASCII file, each alphabetic, numeric, or special character is represented with a 7-binary digit binary number (a string of seven 0s or 1s). 128 possible characters are defined. UNIX and DOS-based operating systems (except for Windows NT) use ASCII for text files. Windows NT uses a newer code, Unicode. IBM's System 390 servers use a proprietary 8-bit code called extended binary-coded decimal interchange code. Conversion programs allow different operating systems to change a file from one code to another.

Baseline: Where the text sits on an imaginary line.

Bins: The output area for cut-sheet paper printers. Multi-bin support is a common requirement in most enterprise printing environments.

Bitmap: This is a raster image. Raster images represent images as bits. This data cannot be indexed unless additional tags are inserted since the data has been turned into pure bits.

Coded Font: An AFP font resource that associates a

code page and a font character set. Prefixed with XO.

Codepage: A font resource that associates code points and character identifiers. Prefixed with T1.

COLD: Computer Output to Laser Disk. This is the generic term for the portion of the industry involved in archiving the print datastream.

Continuous forms printer: A printer that requires continuous forms paper, either on a roll or fan-folded.

CPI: Characters per inch or pitch. Measurement used for fixed pitch fonts.

CRLF: Carriage Return/Line Feed.

Cut-sheet printer: A printer that requires cut-sheet paper, usually in standard letter or legal sizes, or European A4 or B4 sizes.

Daisy-wheel printer: Daisy-wheel printers use a font wheel that contains a single font in a single size. They generally are best for text only.

DBCS: Double-byte character set. Common format for Asian languages.

DJDE (Dynamic Job Descriptor Entry): A resource in a Xerox conditioned line data file or Metacode file that controls a variety of aspects about a print job, including calls to forms, font changes, and information about input bin selection and output tray selection.

Document Composition Facility (DCF): A licensed program (IBM) that provides a text formatter called SCRIPT/VS. SCRIPT/VS can process documents marked up with its own control words as well as documents marked up with GML tags.

DOS/VSE: One of the IBM operating systems.

Dot-matrix printers: Dot-matrix printers use an array of pins to strike an inked printer ribbon that produces images on paper. These printers use either 9 or 24 pins and create each page as a raster image. An increase in pins yields higher quality. These printers are nearly obsolete due to the advent of inkjet printers.

DPI: Dots per inch; print density measurement.

Duplex: Printing on both sides of a sheet of paper.

EBCDIC / extended binary-coded decimal interchange code: A binary code for alphabetic and numeric characters developed by IBM. It is used in IBM's OS/390 operating system. In an EBCDIC file, each alphabetic or numeric character is represented with an 8-bit binary number (a string of eight 0s or 1s). 256 possible characters (letters of the alphabet, numerals, and special characters) are defined.

Electronic Form: This is represented in AFP as an Overlay and in Xerox Metacode/DJDE as an FRM. In PCL and other print languages these are known generically as electronic forms.

EPS: Encapsulated PostScript.

Escape Sequence Languages: Escape code languages are generally characterized by the structure of the commands they use. Each command is prefixed by a special code to signify that the following characters are a command. XES and PCL are Escape Sequence Languages.

FDL: Xerox Forms Description Language. Ther eis also a host-based version, HFDL.

Fixed Pitch Font: A font in which every character uses the same amount of horizontal space. In the scalable fonts most common to Windows-printing there is no such thing as true fixed pitch fonts.

Font: A collection of type characters of a specific style, size, weight, width, and stress. Fonts are the files that provide the artistic interface between the alphanumeric characters in the file and how they are represented on the page (paper or screen). Fonts may be Fixed Pitch or Proportional.

Form: A physical sheet of paper or electronic image onto which data is printed; common terminology in print programming.

GIF: Graphic Interchange Format. A common raster graphic format on the web.

Graphic: The graphics are the artwork that may be a part of the file. The graphic format is unique to the datastream. Graphics may be "raster graphics" which are bitmap representations of the image. Graphics may also be vector graphics, which means that the representation is done in mathematical and syntactical representations of the image. IBM's AFP supports Page Segments (PSEGs) and IOCA raster graphics, as well as GOCA vector graphics. Xerox supports only raster graphics as IMG files. There are also PCL raster graphics, XES/UDK raster graphics, and PostScript raster graphics. There are some independent forms of raster graphics, such as TIFF, PCX, and BMP formats, as well as the GIF format used on the web.

HFDL: Xerox Host Forms Description Language. Used to create Xerox Electronic Forms (FRMs).

Host System: Any computer. We used to use this term to mean only IBM mainframe S/370 or S/390 using an operating system such as MVS or VM to execute application programs. Your host system can now include workstation systems running some form of UNIX, or a workstation running OS/2 or Windows NT.

HTML: HyperText Markup Language. Tag based language interpreted by web browsers.

Image: A pattern of black and white dots that form a picture.

Imposition: A method of laying out pages in a format that causes them to be in the correct order and orientation when the paper is folded.

Inkjet printers: These printers work by ejecting ink through tiny tubes. The ink is heated with tiny resistors or plates that are situated at one end of the tube. The heat actually boils the ink, creating a tiny air bubble that ejects a droplet of ink onto the paper, thus creating portions of the image.

Intelligent Printer Data Stream (IPDS): A device specific printer data stream from IBM, output of PSF.

Interpress: A Xerox interpreted printer data stream, similar in design to PostScript and supported on Xerox ESS printers.

JCL: Job Control Language: Used in an MVS environment.

JDE (Job Descriptor Entry): A Xerox resource that is used to setup the initial job information, such as the DJDE Identifier used in the job. This is a compiled object. The source form is JSL (Job Source Language).

Landscape: Print format where the width of the page is greater than the height.

Laser Printer: A laser printer is a type of computer printer that uses a laser beam to produce an image. The image that is printed consists of an array of very fine dots. The use of the laser in this way allows for the creation of extremely fine dots that can produce detailed images, text, or pictures with a print quality that is similar to the offset printing used to produce books and magazines.

LCDS: Line Conditioned Data Stream used in the Xerox high-speed printing environment.

Leading: The amount of space from baseline to baseline in the printed application.

Line Data: Data prepared for printing on a line printer, such as the IBM 3211 or 1403.

Line Printer: Any printer that accepts and prints one line of text at a time from the host system.

Logical Page: A page structure described within a page printer datastream. One or more logical pages may print on a physical page, as in two-up printing.

Mainframe: The industry term for equipment that conforms to IBM's system 370/390 operating system architecture. We generally think of these as IBM computers, but there are third party vendors such as Hitachi and Amdahl who also make mainframes. Mainframes generally run MVS, VM or DOS/VSE (not the same as MS-DOS) operating systems. For some DEC, Tandem, and Sequoias are also considered mainframes, though we would tend to consider them midrange computers.

Metacode: The name for the Xerox native datastream on their high speed printing systems.

Midrange Computers: These are computers that are generally larger than PCs but smaller than a mainframe... not physically, necessarily, but in terms of computing power.

MO:DCA: Mixed Object Document Content Architecture: This is another description of AFP. It's the architectural description, which has components such as IOCA, GOCA, BCOCA, PTOCA, and FOCA.

Monospaced Font: A font where all characters are the same width; also known as fixed-pitch font.

MVS: Multiple Virtual Storage. One of several operating systems that can be used on IBM and IBM compatible mainframes. MVS uses JCL to cause programs to run and the results of the programs to be printed or routed to storage on hard drives.

Normal Duplex: When printing portrait, pages printed back to back with the tops of the pages at the same end of the paper. When printing landscape, pages printed back to back with the tops of the pages on opposite edges of the paper.

OCX: The deliverable for an ActiveX user. This is a specially compiled form of the program that is usable as an object.

OEM: Original Equipment Manufacturer. We use it to refer to those companies that license our code and build a product around it.

Overlay: A predefined electronic image containing rules, shading, text, boxes, or logos, that can be merged with variable data on a physical page while printing.

Page Description Languages: The page description languages (PDLs) are quite versatile and allow complex pages and images to be created. They are suitable for typographically advanced documents, such as presentations, technical manuals, advertising brochures, and word processing documents.

Parameter File: An external file that tells programs how to treat the file to be transformed. It serves the function of telling the program the things that the printer already knew about the print file format, and passes other environmental information, such as the location of resource (font, form, graphic, control file) files.

PCL: Printer Control Language: This is the HP (Hewlett Packard) architecture that includes PCL 1, 2, 3 4, 5 and 6.

PDA: Personal Digital Assistant: That class of handheld device, like a Palm or Pocket PC device.

PDF / Portable Document Format: PDF (Portable Document Format) is a file format that has captured all the elements of a printed document as an electronic image that you can view, navigate, print, or forward to someone else. PDF files are created using Adobe Acrobat, Acrobat Capture, or similar products. To view and use the files, you need the free Acrobat Reader, which you can easily download. Once you've downloaded the Reader, it will start automatically whenever you want to look at a PDF file.

PNG: portable Network Graphic. Common web graphic format; more robust than GIF.

Portrait: Print format where the height of the page is greater than the width.

PostScript: Adobe's architecture for printing.

PPM: Pages per minute; the speed rating of a printer. Also referred to as images per minute or sheets per minute..

Pre-printed Form: A sheet of paper containing a pre-printed design.

Printer Command Language: Hewlett-Packard (HP) created the Printer Command Language (PCL) to provide an efficient way to control printer features across a number of different printing devices. PCL was originally devised for HP's dot matrix and inkjet printers. The first printer in HP's LaserJet series, the "HP LaserJet" (introduced in 1984), released with the PCL 3 language.

Printer Language: The language used by a printer is the set of commands that it uses to format the data sent from a computer. These commands are embedded within the data and are interpreted by the printer. There are many printer languages, some of which are exclusive to laser printers and others that are designed for older, simpler printers.

Proportional Fonts: These fonts use a different horizontal spacing for each character, more appropriate for text applications.

Raster and Vector Graphics: A raster graphic is an image that is recreated through the use bitmaps. These images are created by printing an array of dots. A vector graphic is an image that is generated using geometrical formulas. This is also known as an object-oriented graphic.

Reports: Generally refers to data produced by application programs in a highly formatted appearance, often using fixed pitch fonts.

Resolution: Resolution refers to the number of dots that can be printed within a specified area. Laser printers construct their images using an array called a "bitmap image". Nearly all laser printers are capable of printing at 300 x 300 dots per square inch (dpi). The typical resolution for most laser output is 600 dpi. Higher-end printers, such as the HP 4000, can achieve 1200 dpi. With the increase in resolution comes better quality, lower print speeds, and increased ink usage.

Resource: A collection of printing instructions such as fonts information, graphics information, and formatting information, which can be called by a program as needed.

Rotation: The orientation of a character in relation to the print direction.

SCRIPT: A formatting program used by DCF and BookMaster for processing text.

SGML: Standard Generalized Markup Language: ISO standard for document source interchange.

Simplex: Printing on only one side of the paper.

Transforms: These are any of our products that change one type of file into some other format.

Trays: The input hopper for paper. Some equipment supports multiple input bins which may be controlled from the print applications or control files

Tumble Duplex: When printing portrait, pages printed back to back with the tops of the pages on opposite ends of the paper. When printing landscape, pages printed back to back with the tops of the pages printed on the same edge of the paper.

Typeface: All type of a single family. Many fonts of different sizes may have the same typeface.

UDK: User Defined Key. See XES.

UNIX: An operating system that comes in many flavors. IBM sells AIX as their form of UNIX. SUN sells both SUN OS and SUN Solaris as their (mutually incompatible) versions of UNIX. HP sells HP-UX as their form of UNIX. We support all of these forms. In addition there are other forms of UNIX which we do not currently support, such as SINIX (Siemens, though the AIX version works on some SINIX systems), SCO UNIX (Santa Cruz Operation UNIX), and Bell Labs (the originators of UNIX) Unix V.

Unprintable Area: The area of a sheet of paper where no printing can be done due to printer-hardware limitations, usually a thin strip around the edges of the sheet of paper.

VM: Virtual Machine. One of the operating systems that run on an IBM mainframe.

XES: Xerox Escape Sequence. Another name for UDK, the decentralized Xerox printing format.

XML: eXtensible Markup Language. An architecture for defining tags used within data files.

Why not collect all of the MC² books?

Designing a Document Strategy
by Kevin Craine

Designing a Document Strategy targets managers, technicians and consultants who see the benefit and cost savings inherent in implementing a document strategy. The clearly defined five-phase process can be tailored to any environment. It includes Cause-effect diagrams, flow charts, and ROI formulas that can be copied and put into use. Case examples demonstrate application of the theories in the real world, leading to meaningful and informed action. Regardless of their final recommendations, readers will be more likely to bring about real-world, bottom-line benefits. There is no better educational resource on designing a document strategy than this book.

Only $29.95
plus shipping

Critical Mass: A Primer for Living with the Future
by Pat McGrew & Bill McDaniel

Every manager faces the technology squeeze. Adopt too early and the executives question your sanity. Adopt too late and you're called a dinosaur. Now a quick-to-read primer can help you make better decisions on the road to the future. There is no better resource for anyone who feels overwhelmed by the rapid pace of change and needs to find a baseline to understand how we evolved to where we are today. This easy-to-read set of essays arms the reader with an overview of the evolution of technology. Remember Jane Jetson? Star Trek? Frank Gilbreth or Cheaper By The Dozen? War of the Worlds? Critical Mass essays re-visit these members of the technology cast as well as the invention of the keyboard, wearable computing innovations, and the future of interactive TV.

Only $15.00
plus shipping

To order, visit our website at www.mcgrewmcdaniel.com! OR, call us at +1 817 577 8984 and we'll be happy to take your order over the phone. We accept faxed Corporate Purchase Orders at +1 817 577 9371. And, don't forget to ask about our bulk purchase discounts!

www.ingramcontent.com/pod-product-compliance
Lightning Source LLC
LaVergne TN
LVHW042333060326
832902LV00006B/139

* 9 781893 347021 *